ALL IN

THE STORY OF LeBRON JAMES
AND THE 2016 NBA CHAMPION
CLEVELAND CAVALIERS

VINCE McKEE

SPORTS
PUBLISHING

Sports Publishing books may be purchased in bulk at special discounts for sales promotion, corporate gifts, fund-raising, or educational purposes. Special editions can also be created to specifications. For details, contact the Special Sales Department, Sports Publishing, 307 West 36th Street, 11th Floor, New York, NY 10018 or sportspubbooks@ skyhorsepublishing.com.

Sports Publishing® is a registered trademark of Skyhorse Publishing, Inc.®, a Delaware corporation.

Visit our website at www.sportspubbooks.com.

10 9 8 7 6 5 4 3 2 1

Library of Congress Cataloging-in-Publication Data is available on file.

Cover design by Tom Lau
Cover photo credit: AP Images

ISBN: 978-1-68358-074-4
Ebook ISBN: 978-1-68358-075-1

Printed in the United States of America

This book is dedicated to my bean, and my best little buddy, my beautiful daughter and best friend, my daughter, Maggie! You will forever be the best daughter a daddy could ever ask for!

Contents

Acknowledgments

I WOULD LIKE TO THANK Emily, my wife and driving force. Your support and willingness to let me chase this dream have allowed me to reach levels of success I never thought possible. For every feature on ESPN and *SLAM* Magazine, to every dinner at home with you and the Bean, they all bring me joy. You were with me way back when I mailed out countless query letters for *Hero*, desperately trying to get my little book filled with dreams picked up.

It has happened, God has blessed our lives with more success and love than I ever thought possible, and I thank you for helping me believe it was possible in the first place. From the floor of Parma Woods apartment stamping countless envelopes to the kitchen table feeding macaroni and cheese to Maggie, you have been there with me every step of the journey and I will always love you for it! May our love forever grow and continue to teach others the values of partnership and that through the power of God all things are possible.

I would like to thank my parents, Don and Maria McKee. You have always been there for me since day one and have always been my biggest supporters. You knew when I was a little boy how badly I wanted to be a writer and how badly I wanted to celebrate a Cleveland championship. Through the struggles of life and the ups and downs, you have never let me stop believing in myself. Can you believe we have gotten this far, can you believe I give speeches at schools and libraries and churches? Can you believe I've been featured in *SLAM* Magazine and on ESPN? It's no longer a dream but a reality, and I owe so much of it to you both. Thank you for loving my daughter Maggie the way you do. She is such a good girl, and I can't wait until September 2016, when she becomes a big sister.

Thank you to my cousin James Friguglietti, who has been my guiding light during this incredible five-year journey I have been on. If it weren't for your help in the beginning as I wrote *Hero*, I'm not sure I could have ever pulled it off. Maybe someday with your help, I can write your epic story?

Thank you to my brother, Donald, sister-in-law, Abbie, and nephew, Matthew. I miss you guys terribly and look forward to your visits "up north." As with Mom and Dad, you saw me when I was lost years ago, but never gave up hope I'd get it turned around one day.

Thank you to Ken Carman, Emmett Golden, Nick Camino, Jerry Mires, Bruce Drennan, and Sam Bourquin for having me on your radio shows to promote my books when absolutely no one else would. Thank you to Kenny Roda, not only for the pictures in the book, but also for your friendship over the years. I never thought the guy I would look forward to hearing everyday on the radio would be on speed dial next to Kenny Lofton in my phone.

Thank you to West Park UCC for also allowing me to feature my work and supporting me.

Thank you to my late great uncle, Peter DeLuca, for instilling the flame of writing and creating in me as a four-year-old little boy. You, along with my Uncle Jimmy, were always my toughest critics but also men of honor and inspiration who never let me give up. You're never far away from me in heart and soul when I write.

Last, but certainly not least, thank you to my lord and savior Jesus Christ. It is through your light that all work is done.

Prologue: Six Days Later

June 25, 2016

IT HAS BEEN SIX DAYS and nights since the Cavaliers shocked the world and won the NBA Finals on Sunday night, June 19. It was Father's Day, and the Cavaliers gave every father in Northeast Ohio the greatest gift they possibly could. In so many ways it still seems all so surreal, almost as if it were a dream, but it wasn't and the joy is real, very real!

The Cavaliers ended Cleveland's fifty-two-year drought without a championship on the heels of one of the most dramatic and controversial seasons ever. They ran though the play-offs, losing only twice in the first three rounds, before dropping three of their first four games against 73-win Golden State before finally catching fire and destiny. The Cavaliers played as if they had nothing to lose, and there was no stopping them as they found their stride and confidence over the final three games of the finals.

So here we are, six days later, and I couldn't be more proud of this great city we call home on the shores of Lake Erie. We have survived every kind of sports pain one could imagine, but it was all worth it, all a part of our destiny. We had LeBron James, basketball's best player, join our team straight from high school, a hometown boy who was seen as the savior. He broke our hearts by leaving us in July of 2010. But in many ways, that may have just been the greatest thing ever to happen to Cleveland sports.

By James leaving, it allowed the Cavaliers to draft first only one year later. That draft pick was Kyrie Irving, the same man who hit the championship-winning shot over league MVP Stephen Curry. A few years later when the Cavaliers were still rebuilding, they were blessed to draft first two years in a row, selecting Anthony Bennett and then Andrew Wiggins. Those four years of hell were worth it, as those two draft picks, Bennett and Wiggins, were used as trade bait to acquire Kevin Love—the same Kevin Love who defended brilliantly against Steph Curry in the waning seconds of Game Seven, not allowing him a clean look at a game-tying three-pointer.

If LeBron James doesn't leave Cleveland, there isn't any Kevin Love to make the stop. If LeBron James doesn't leave Cleveland, there isn't Kyrie Irving to hit the championship-clinching, drought-ending, curse-stomping three-pointer! If LeBron James doesn't leave Cleveland, then there aren't 1.3 million people attending an all-day-long championship parade and rally.

You see, Cleveland, a wise man once said, is "hell" getting to "heaven." You have lived it firsthand, and now in a matter of thirty days you have seen a UFC Heavyweight Champion in Stipe Miocic. You have seen an AHL Calder Cup championship team in the Lake Erie Monsters. And now, perhaps the sweetest gift of all from the basketball gods, the Cleveland Cavaliers have won the 2016 NBA championship. Celebrate this championship like you have the last six days for the rest of your life. For this championship isn't just for the players, it is for you, too! It is for every blue-collar worker who goes through forty hours of hell each week to put food on the table for his family. This championship is for every person who ever believed in miracles. This championship is for you!

Introduction

THE CAVALIERS HAD BEEN IN basketball hell for four consecutive seasons from 2010 to 2014. On July 10, 2010, their "Chosen One," LeBron James, had left the city on national television during a live interview with Jim Gray on ESPN for his infamous "Decision." This caused a nationwide backlash against James, causing him to go from one of the most beloved athletes in sports, to one of the most hated in the blink of an eye. After failing to win a championship while playing for the Cavaliers, he chose to leave Cleveland and form a super team in Miami with fellow 2003 draft All Stars and close friends, Dwyane Wade and Chris Bosh.

Broadcast from the Boys and Girls Club of Greenwich, Connecticut, on ESPN, the program started at 9:00 p.m., but it wasn't until twenty-eight minutes into the show that James finally announced his decision to play for the Miami Heat and join fellow All-Stars Wade and Bosh. Cleveland fans were shocked and devastated.

The Cavaliers endured four horrible seasons and failed to attract any big-name free agents. The general feeling was that players would not want to play for Cleveland owner Dan Gilbert because of the way he spoke out against James's leaving. It was unheard of for an owner to speak his mind and reflect the emotions of the long-suffering fans in the egocentric superstar world of the NBA. Gilbert might have been correct to do so, but he would eventually pay for it.

The promise of a title would eventually come true for James in his second season in Miami, as the Heat would win back-to-back titles against the Oklahoma City Thunder in 2012 and the San Antonio Spurs in 2013. James arguably had his best two seasons as a pro during those campaigns and garnered his third and fourth NBA MVP awards in the process, along with being voted MVP of the Finals both times. He was playing the best basketball of his life, but he wasn't doing it in Northeast Ohio.

Things would begin to change in 2014 as the Heat once again took on the San Antonio Spurs in the NBA Finals. Suddenly, Wade was hurt, the Heat looked old and slow, and James was a one-man show with little to no help. That was the same reason he had left Cleveland four seasons prior. It was clear that James had come full circle, and after the Spurs knocked off the Heat four games to one, James was at a crossroads in his career.

LeBron James had an option in his contract to opt out of it and become a free agent. When asked in the post-series press conference about his plans for the offseason and if he would opt out of his contract early, he was noncommittal and simply stated that he needed to spend time with his family. Rumors would begin to fly, some believing he might leave, most believing he would stay. James answered all the questions himself on July 11 in an essay with *Sports Illustrated* columnist Lee Jenkins, making the official announcement that the King was coming home, and a new era of basketball in Cleveland was set to begin.

LeBron would be coming home, and the Cavaliers would strive to build a dream team around him once again. Would it happen, could they really win it all? As we all know in life, nothing is guaranteed, and the city of Cleveland would find that out firsthand as one of the most epic and hard-fought runs to a title was set to begin.

CHAPTER 1

A Look Back

ON THE MORNING OF JULY 12, 2014, virtually every sports fan in Cleveland woke up and immediately pinched themselves. Did it really happen the day before, did the chosen one really decide to come back home? It almost seemed too good to be true. The Cavaliers and their fans had just survived four brutal years of hell, while also watching LeBron James, the kid who grew up in front of their eyes only to bolt for Miami, win two NBA Championships and appear in four straight NBA Finals.

Suddenly, the prodigal son had returned and all of the hate for him disappeared. Within hours of the announcement of James coming home to Cleveland, season tickets sold out at Quicken Loans Arena. There was no denying the excitement of Cavaliers fans. It appeared that all was forgiven, and the rebuilding of a Cleveland dynasty was now in place.

LeBron James would be joining up with one of the best young players in the NBA, point guard Kyrie Irving, who was about to enter his fourth season with the Cavaliers. The one-two punch of James and Irving already had fans dreaming of a championship and salivating at the thought of this dream team starting to take instant shape. Perhaps they could even add a third superstar member and hand Cleveland a Big Three of their own.

General manager David Griffin would take on the same task as Danny Ferry had years before him of building a championship-caliber team around his star player, LeBron James. He knew the dynamic duo of James and Irving would be potent, but the NBA was in the era of the "Big Three," and he would have to keep his eyes open for the last important piece, or so he thought.

Griffin was no stranger to the sport, and people close to him would confirm that he lived and breathed basketball. He got his first taste at the pro level in the early 1990s, when he became the tournament director for the Nike Desert Classic pre-draft camp. He also spent time on the bench as a coach, serving as an assistant at Scottsdale Community College.

He came to the Cavs with seventeen years of experience with the Phoenix Suns. He began his front office career with the Suns as an intern in 1993. Griffin showed that hard work and loyalty can pay off when he was named senior vice president of basketball operations for Phoenix in 2007. He joined the Cavaliers before the 2010–11 season as vice president of basketball operations before being named general manager in February of 2014. Sometimes a GM or president is only as good as his coach, and Griffin would have to go to the dance with a rookie on the bench.

The man in charge of the hefty task of controlling and coaching the new dream roster was David Blatt. Griffin had decided to fire the previous coach, Mike Brown, at the close of the prior season. Griffin felt that the team needed an offensive-minded coach that could mold the Cavaliers to play more like the Lenny Wilkens–led teams of the late-'80s and early-'90s that were known for their ball movement. He interviewed several candidates including former players Mark Price, Tyronn Lue, and Alvin Gentry before finding his man in David Blatt.

Blatt was a head coaching icon in the Euroleague for many years and was offered a reported four-year deal worth a whopping $20 million to coach the Cavaliers and pass up an assistant coaching position with the Golden State Warriors. Blatt, fifty-five, was the first coach to make the leap from Europe to the NBA as a head coach. Gilbert and general manager David Griffin chose Blatt over Lue, an assistant with the Los Angeles Clippers. It was a decision that would eventually haunt all three men for a long time.

One of the most successful European coaches of this era, Blatt resigned from his job as the championship coach of Maccabi Tel Aviv to pursue his longtime goal of coaching in the NBA. Blatt was born and raised in Massachusetts, playing his college basketball for Hall of Famer Pete Carill at Princeton before embarking on a hugely successful head coaching career overseas.

Blatt coached undermanned Macabbi Tel Aviv to a dramatic upset victory over Real Madrid for the Euroleague championship in 2014. Blatt had tremendous success across two decades overseas. He led the Russian national team to the 2007 Eurobasket championship and a bronze medal in the 2012 London Olympics. As impressive as his overseas coaching career was, in Cleveland he would still have to contend all year with reporters who called him a "rookie coach," a term that angered Blatt every time he heard it. He was never hesitant to remind anyone of his time coaching overseas. He was brought to Cleveland at first thinking it would be a young, unproven team in need of growth that he would be coaching. Within weeks, things changed, and his low pressure job became pressure-packed.

Blatt would need to rely heavily on a strong relationship with Kyrie Irving, his new point guard, if the team was to have any success. Meanwhile, Griffin was about to pull the trigger on a deal to get him some help. Rumors had been flying since LeBron James came back to town that Cleveland would find a way to get Minnesota Timberwolves superstar forward Kevin Love. Soon the rumors would turn into reality.

As part of a three-team trade on August 23, the Cavaliers traded a 2015 first-round draft pick to the Philadelphia 76ers; they also traded Anthony Bennett, Andrew Wiggins, and a trade exception to the Minnesota Timberwolves for Kevin Love. Minnesota shipped Luc Mbah a Moute and Alexey Shved to Philadelphia; and Philadelphia sent Thaddeus Young to Minnesota.

The deal boiled down to Love for Wiggins, a 6'8" forward from Kansas who was the first overall selection in the 2014 NBA draft. It didn't seem like the Timberwolves were willing to entertain trade talks until Love withdrew from the 2014 FIBA Basketball World Cup team because he knew a deal with the Cavaliers was suddenly possible after LeBron James returned. Love had been one of the most dominant power forwards in the Western Conference since being drafted by Minnesota in 2008 from UCLA with the fifth overall pick. A three-time all-star, he was seen as the final piece of the dream team that would give Cleveland its first major sports championship since 1954.

Kevin Love was named to the All-NBA Second Team twice (2012 and 2014), was voted the NBA's Most Improved Player in 2011, and was an NBA All-Rookie Second Team selection in 2009. He was also won the NBA Three-Point Shootout in 2012 and led the league in rebounding in 2011. In college, he was Consensus first-team All-American and Pac-10 Player of the Year.

The reason for so much drama and surprise surrounding the Love trade was that he been quoted as saying numerous times that if the Cavaliers traded for him, he would opt out of his contract once he got the chance. Now that LeBron James was a Cavalier once again, the thought was that Love would re-sign with the team and not opt out of the contract, thus making the Cavaliers front office feel better about trading away Wiggins for him.

Love was coming off of his best season with the Timberwolves as he averaged 26 points and 12.5 rebounds a game. It was a risky move for the Cavaliers because they had to part with not only Wiggins, but also Bennett, the first overall pick from the previous season. The Cavaliers took the ultimate gamble getting rid of the top pick in the draft before he could even play a single game for them. They were "all in" with Kevin Love. They reasoned that Wiggins hadn't played a single professional game yet and Bennett was a giant bust in his rookie season. It was a calculated risk but went with the win-now attitude they were taking on.

As the Cavaliers approached training camp with a near dream team, expectations were high for the first time in many years. They had their Big Three of James, Love, and Irving, and if they could mesh quickly and stay healthy, some pundits predicted they could win 70 games. They had their way with everyone they faced in preseason, even playing against James's former team, the Miami Heat, in a preseason game held in Brazil. The simple fact, however, was that preseason basketball doesn't mean anything and they would have to do it in the regular season on a nightly basis, or everyone would consider them a gigantic failure. They knew that the second something went wrong, people would be jumping off the bandwagon and looking to bury them. Little did anyone realize just how often that would end up happening and just how many steep challenges the Cavaliers would end up having to face.

The Cavaliers came in with a strong starting five but had little in the way of a bench, and that was the one thing that kept certain media outlets and publications from picking the

Cavaliers to go all the way. Their opening night roster consisted of a starting backcourt of Kyrie Irving at point guard with Dion Waiters at shooting guard. Waiters played his best ball coming off the bench, but his ego demanded a starting spot on the "dream" roster. It wouldn't last long. The forwards were LeBron James and Kevin Love, with Anderson Varejao in the middle.

To the surprise of everyone, things did not go as well as they hoped, and they got off to a shaky start. By Christmas, they were only 17–11 and already showing signs of cracking. Their woes really began on Christmas Day in Miami. They trailed the Heat throughout the game, and LeBron's former teammates were out for blood. The Cavaliers lost, 101–91, in a game where James and Irving combined for 55 points, but no one else did nearly enough to help.

The real drama unfolded after the game when LeBron was caught on camera and microphone saying to Wade, "If this thing doesn't work out, we'll get back at it next year and do it better than ever next time." That one quote sent the entire NBA world into a frenzy, and the city of Cleveland into a panic.

With paranoia at an all-time high about LeBron James once again possibly leaving, he did his best to quell worries and led the Cavaliers past the Orlando Magic the next night in Orlando, 98–89. The good feelings wouldn't last long, however, as they went on to lose nine of their next ten games. General manager David Griffin did not panic; instead, he decided to pull the trigger on deals that would save the season.

On January 5, 2015, they acquired J. R. Smith in the hopes that his shooting range would return and his maturity level would increase with the move to a new city with less room to get in trouble. As part of a three-team trade, the Cavaliers traded Dion Waiters to the Oklahoma City Thunder; they also traded Louis Amundson, Alex Kirk, and a 2019 second-round draft pick to the

New York Knicks. The Knicks traded Iman Shumpert and J. R. Smith to the Cleveland Cavaliers, and the Thunder traded their 2015 first-round draft pick to the Cavaliers and Lance Thomas to the New York Knicks.

It was a huge risk for the Cavaliers because they had put so much time into developing Waiters, but it was apparent he was not going to succeed in Blatt's ball movement–style offense that LeBron excelled in. Waiters had shown flashes of skill but was considered a cancer in the locker room and couldn't make a shot off the ball: he had to have the ball passed to him so he could set and shoot. The Cavs needed guys who create shots, not wait for the ball like Waiters had done so many times. It was clear that Waiters was not in the plans going forward. They felt that if they could get anything from Smith and Shumpert as far as an outside threat and increased defense went, the trade would be worth it.

The trade took place during part of a stretch with LeBron out on a minivacation to get his mind, body, and soul correct. By the time he returned on Tuesday, January 13, against the Phoenix Suns after missing eight games, the Cavaliers were 19–19 and in desperate need of a win. They wouldn't get one, as the Suns ruined James's first game back and put the Cavaliers away, 107–100. Cleveland dropped under .500 with their sixth consecutive loss and had everyone in the media and fans at home talking about the rumored dismissal of head coach David Blatt. General manager David Griffin would hear none of it and stood behind his coach. He was about to be rewarded for his faith.

With sixteen games left before the All Star break, the Cavs had a little over three weeks to get things turned around in the right direction. It was almost as if they realized play time was over and it was time to get serious as they began an epic run. Starting at Los Angeles against the Lakers on January 15, they won twelve straight games, an impressive run that featured several incredible performances. They beat both the Lakers and Clippers on the road to get it started. They followed that up with consecutive home wins against the Chicago Bulls, Utah Jazz, Charlotte Hornets, and Oklahoma City Thunder. They went into the Palace of Auburn Hills and beat the Detroit Pistons before heading back home to topple the Portland Trail Blazers in a game that saw Kyrie Irving score 55 points.

They remained hot in the second half of the season following the break and suddenly became one of the best teams in basketball, as they finished the 2014–15 regular season with a 53–29 record. It was a mark good enough for the second-best record in the Eastern Conference. Despite having a lesser record than the top-seeded Atlanta Hawks, the red-hot Cavaliers were the popular pick to reach the NBA Finals. Their talent was coming together and starting to mesh at the perfect time.

The Cavaliers were looking like a serious threat to win the NBA championship as they headed into the 2015 playoffs. The only questions were the lack of experience of so many key figures. Coach David Blatt had never coached in a NBA playoff game and two of their three best players, Love and Irving, had no postseason experience. Little did anyone know that playoff experience would be the least of their concerns, and the nation was about to see how much of an actual "team" this squad truly was.

Their first-round opponent was the seventh-seeded Boston Celtics. Cleveland had struggled mightily against the men in green in past playoff matchups. The Celtics had knocked LeBron and the Cavaliers out of the playoffs twice during James's first stint in Cleveland. This Celtics team was different, much younger and less talented than in the past. Gone were stars such as Ray Allen, Kevin Garnett, and Paul Pierce. This version was made up of young guns like forward Jeff Green, who averaged 17.6 points a game. The Celtics also had sharpshooter Evan Turner, whom many Cavaliers fans were very familiar with from his time playing at Ohio State. Another Boston player to keep an eye on would be point guard Isaiah Thomas, who was averaging a team-high 19 points a game to go along with 5.4 assists.

The Celtics finished at 41–41 and split the season series with the Cavaliers. The two games they won were highly forgettable, however, because they came in the final week of the season. One of the losses came in a game in which four of Cleveland's regular starters did not play, and the other in which they only played a few minutes of the first half.

The Celtics had been pretty much left for dead after star point guard Rajon Rondo was traded away earlier in the season. But under the control of their visionary young head coach Brad Stevens, the Celtics never gave up and put together a late-season playoff push. Stevens had come into his own coaching college ball at Butler University. He led the Bulldogs to back-to-back NCAA championship games out of the lightly-regarded Horizon League conference. Stevens and the Bulldogs lost both title games, to Duke in 2010 and then UConn in 2011. In the summer of 2013, Stevens took the job with the Celtics, at the age of thirty-six, becoming one of the youngest head coaches in NBA history. The Celtics went 40–42 in their first season under Stevens, good enough to reach the playoffs as a seventh seed, before getting knocked off by LeBron James and the Miami Heat in convincing fashion. Despite how well Stevens had coached, his team would still be a heavy underdog against the Cavs.

Heading into the 2015 NBA playoffs, Kyrie Irving had always been a big money player, at his best when the lights were on the brightest. He had already won Most Valuable Player honors at the 2014 NBA All-Star Game and the 2014 FIBA World Cup. He also won the 2014 NBA All-Star Weekend Three-Point Shootout and continued to be one of the best point guards in the game. Some did question how well he would play in his first NBA playoff game, but Irving wasted no time quieting his critics by making his first five three-point attempts, scoring 20 points in 21 first-half minutes as the Celtics were desperate for answers on how to stop him. Irving would finish with 30 points, three rebounds, and two assists in Cleveland's 113–100 victory.

LeBron James added 20 points, seven assists, six rebounds, two steals and a block in his return to playoff action with the Cleveland Cavaliers. His last playoff game with Cleveland back in 2010 was also against Boston and brought a bitter end to his first stay in Cleveland. Once he arrived in Miami, he learned how to beat the Celtics and led the Heat past them in three straight playoff seasons.

Kevin Love did his part to uphold his place in the Big Three, as he made his final three field-goal attempts and finished with 19 points, 12 rebounds, four assists, and a steal in 33 minutes in his first career playoff game. The postseason debuts for Love, Irving, and head coach David Blatt were successful ones. The same could be said for Sixth Man of the Year candidate Tristan Thompson, who also worked his tail off and pulled down six rebounds off the bench with 12 crucial points and an assist.

The Celtics hung tough all night and led for most of the first half before the Cavs found their playoff stride. Isaiah Thomas led the Celtics with 22 points off the bench and his sharpshooting kept them in it. To Stevens's credit, the Celtics did not just roll over for the big bad Cavaliers. They showed right away that this would be a tough, hard-fought series.

Game Two was a back-and-forth affair for the entire first half and most of the second half. The Cavaliers did just enough to pull away from the Celtics and go up 2–0 in their first-round series with a 99–91 victory. LeBron led the way by scoring 30 points, pulling down nine rebounds, and dishing out seven assists.

He had an incredible fourth quarter with 15 points to help the Cavaliers pull away with the win. During the game, he passed Jerry "The Logo" West on the all-time NBA playoff scoring list. He did have 11 turnovers in the two games, so he would have to clean that up as the series would go on the road.

Kyrie Irving, the star of the series opener, also had a big night with 26 points, six assists, and five rebounds. Timofey Mozgov did exactly what the Cavaliers traded for him to do, as he was a dominant presence all night long in the middle. Despite playing most of the game in foul trouble (he would eventually foul out), Mozgov was a monster on the boards, ripping down seven rebounds, and also had an incredible five blocked shots along with a career playoff high 16 points.

While only scoring seven points, J. R. Smith also put his work in on the defensive side of the ball by making five steals and leading the Cavaliers on several fast breaks. They trailed by as many as nine late in the first half before they rallied late to actually hold a 51–50 lead going into the half, thanks in part to a very strong showing by Kevin Love, who refused to be denied and attacked the rim all night long. Love scored almost all of his 13 points in the rally.

Cleveland stayed hot and built a double-digit lead in the second half before a raucous crowd at Quicken Loans Arena. Not to be overlooked was Tristan Thompson, who again came up big off the bench with 11 rebounds.

The Celtics got another big effort out of Isaiah Thomas with 22 points off the bench. Boston did have four other players score in double digits, but in the end, it was not enough.

After getting off to slow starts in the first halves of the first two games in the series, Cleveland's high-powered offense finally woke up in Boston in a 103–95 win. Unlike the first two games where the Cavs looked sluggish and sloppy early on, they came out hot and aggressive in the early moments of Game Three at the TD Garden. It was crucial for Cleveland to start hot because the crowd in Boston was raucous, and if they fell behind early, the loud crowd may have not let them come back as they did in the first two contests.

In a game in which the Cavaliers finally won a first quarter in this series, they would take a 56–48 lead into halftime, with LeBron James scoring the last nine points of the half. They kept up the momentum in the third quarter and didn't allow the Celtics to crawl back into the game, as they maintained the eight-point lead heading into the final frame. In true championship fashion, the Cavaliers did not allow the boys from Beantown to breathe, as they put things away in the fourth quarter courtesy of Love's game-clinching corner three-pointer with 27 seconds left. LeBron James had his best showing of the playoffs as he scored 31 points, pulled down 11 rebounds, and handed out four assists while stealing the ball four times and blocking two shots. This massive effort from James came on the heels of his publicly supporting his head coach David Blatt for the first time all season. It truly looked like this Cavs team was coming together and improving every game.

With Kyrie Irving guarded heavily all night long by a scrappy Celtics defense, the Cavs found Love more than willing and able to step in as the second scoring threat behind James. Love finished with 23 points and nine rebounds and knocked down several key three-pointers that stopped a couple of Celtics rallies. Love looked—and played—like a max contract player when it mattered most. Game Four and a possible sweep awaited, and if they could only get out of it injury free and on to the next round, things would be looking good—if only!

Canadian-born Kelly Olynyk was a mere NBA footnote until April 26, 2015, when he would enter basketball infamy. Olynyk came from a basketball family, as his father, Ken, was head men's basketball coach at the University of Toronto from 1989 to 2002 and the Canadian junior men's national team from 1983 to 1996. Following that stint he became athletic director at Thompson Rivers University in Kamloops, British Columbia.

His mother was also around the game, as she worked as a Canadian Interuniversity Sport women's basketball referee. NBA basketball was in his blood, since his mother also worked in several roles for the Toronto Raptors from 1996 to 2004. Olynyk would erase the legacy in one afternoon.

Game Four was a wild affair that saw ejections and star players go down to injury, but the Cavs managed to hang on and beat the Celtics, 101–93, to complete a sweep and advance to the Eastern Conference semis. The contest didn't come without several incidents: Kevin Love suffered a horrific shoulder injury early in the first quarter with the Cavs up, 18–10. He was going for a rebound when he got tangled up with Olynyk, who hung on to Love's arm and yanked it downward. Love suffered a separated shoulder that would keep him out of the rest of the playoffs and require surgery, causing instant panic throughout the Cavaliers franchise and the city of Cleveland. Just like that, in one very dirty play, the Cavaliers' chances of winning a title all but disappeared. Love was among many who claimed it was intentional on the part of Olynyk, who received a one-game suspension.

The Cavs didn't allow Love's injury to stop them, as they dominated Boston throughout the first half and the start of the third quarter to build a 21-point lead. The drama didn't stop; the rough play would continue several times in that run. Late in the second quarter, after Jae Crowder gave Cavs swingman Iman Shumpert a shot going up the court, the Boston forward found himself on the receiving end of a stiff screen from Cleveland center Kendrick Perkins. Crowder hit the deck from the hard shot and a mêlée ensued once he got up.

At the start of the second half with the Cavs looking to build on a 21-point lead, J. R. Smith and Crowder battled for a rebound when things again got out of hand as Crowder laid in several stiff shots to the back of Smith. Smith responded by rearing back and swinging his right arm backward, clocking Crowder right on the jaw. Crowder crumpled to the floor following the punch, with his left knee trapped underneath him. As he lay on the hardwood, he reached for his left leg in pain.

After reviewing the play, the referees deemed Smith's swing to constitute "unnecessary and excessive" contact, meriting a flagrant foul 2 and an automatic ejection. The Celtics used the ejections and injuries to play inspired basketball, along with questionable officiating, to close the gap late in the final quarter and narrow the lead to only six points in the closing moments. The Cavs hung on and advanced, but the price they paid for the victory was costly. Love had averaged 14.3 points per game in the series, and now he was lost for the rest of the playoffs.

The Cavaliers, as they did all season, entered the second round of the playoffs against the Chicago Bulls facing extreme adversity. Their starting shooting guard, J. R. Smith, would be suspended for the first two games of the series after his dirty play in Game Four against Boston. Even more serious was the fact that they had lost Kevin Love, one of their three best players, for the remainder of the season. Cleveland had eight days to prepare for Chicago between series, but it wasn't enough, as the Bulls took game one at Quicken Loans Arena by a score of 99–92.

Game Two belonged to the Cavaliers from the opening tip to the final buzzer: they dominated the Bulls all night long en route to a 106–91 victory. Tristan Thompson was inserted into the starting lineup for this one, and the towering Canadian didn't disappoint, collecting 12 rebounds in 35 hard-fought minutes. The series was even after two lopsided games, and the real drama was about to start.

Headed to Chicago with the series knotted up at one game apiece, tensions were on high alert, as the rowdy Chicago crowd was determined to will the Bulls on to victory. They did exactly that: the game was tied in the closing seconds when Derrick Rose hit a buzzer-beating three-point shot to give the Bulls a 99–96 victory. It was a heartbreaking loss for the Cavaliers on the road.

It was also the first game that Cavaliers fans and Kyrie Irving's teammates sensed something might be wrong with him. He was a shell of himself all game and only scored 11 points with two turnovers. It was later revealed that Irving was battling severe tendinitis in his right knee and foot. He would never truly recover.

The Cavaliers, down 2–1, were in desperation mode heading into Game Four in Chicago two days later. The Bulls led throughout most of the game until the Cavaliers made an incredible comeback midway through the fourth quarter to take an 80–73 lead with under four minutes to go. That is when J. R. Smith committed a foolish technical foul that changed the momentum of the game and allowed the Bulls to storm back, eventually tying the game at 84 apiece with nine seconds to go. Rose hit the tying basket after LeBron James was called for an offensive foul.

The drama only increased from there, as David Blatt tried calling a timeout the Cavaliers didn't have. Luckily for Cleveland, the referees didn't notice it, or else it would have resulted in a technical foul. LeBron drove the lane and was fouled trying to take the winning layup, but the refs chose not to call the clear foul and instead awarded the ball out of bounds to the Cavaliers. It was at this moment that the referees called a timeout of their own to review the final play and make sure they had the correct amount of time left on the clock. While all the mayhem was going on, Blatt called a play from the sidelines with his team, but it involved LeBron inbounding the ball and someone else taking the final shot. James didn't agree and decided to change the play in the huddle.

It was gutsy but the coach let him do it, and it was a good thing that he did, because seconds later, James hit a 21-footer from the corner after taking the inbound pass from Matthew Dellavedova to win the game for the Cavaliers, 86–84, and silence the deafening Chicago crowd. It was as clutch a performance from LeBron as you can ask from an athlete. The game-winner capped off a 25 point, 14 rebound, eight assist night, yet another near triple-double for James. The Cavs needed his great effort, as the banged-up Irving continued to struggle, scoring only 12 points. One point of worry was the fact that LeBron didn't even try to hide the fact that he changed the play and made a point of talking about it in the post-game press conference.

Jimmy Butler scored 29 points for the Bulls in Game Five back in Cleveland, but it wasn't enough as the Cavaliers prevailed, 106–101. Chicago overcame a nine-point deficit at the start of the fourth quarter, but the Cavaliers woke up long enough to climb back ahead for the win. Irving returned to form as he scored 25 points in a superb effort. Not bad for a guy pretty much playing on one leg. Irving also dished out five assists. The series was now headed back to Chicago with the Cavaliers up, 3–2, and having a chance to put the Bulls away for good. The Cavs smelled the blood in the water and were ready to keep attacking.

Matthew Dellavedova was born in Australia with the dream of one day playing professional basketball in the United States. He played his college ball at Saint Mary's College of California but went undrafted. He would realize his dream when he joined the Cleveland Cavaliers for the 2013 NBA Summer League. In late 2013, he signed a two-year, $1.3 million contract with the Cavaliers.

After a subpar rookie season, he would receive another chance, as David Blatt liked what he saw in him from the first minutes of summer camp in 2014. Even with the Big Three and multiple big-name free agent veterans the Cavaliers brought in, Blatt knew he had something in Dellavedova, since he liked his aggressive nonstop energy on defense, where he could get even the most seasoned shooters riled up.

His stats were nothing to write home about, only 4.8 points and three assists per game. It was what he brought to the team that wasn't on a stat sheet that truly made the difference, since his heart and hustle were unmatched. This was never more the case than during Game Six in Chicago, when he scored a team-high 19 points to help the Cavaliers defeat the Bulls and advance to the conference finals for the first time since 2009. Irving left the game early in the first quarter with an injury, and Dellavedova stepped up. The Cleveland Cavaliers, once a team left for dead without Kevin Love, were now headed to the Eastern Conference Finals against the top-seeded Atlanta Hawks. The confidence of the team and their fans was at an all-time high. The entire city of Cleveland was on a mission to return to the NBA Finals since the day LeBron James came back home. The Hawks had the best record in the East and had beaten the Cavs soundly in three of the four meetings during the regular season. Cleveland wasn't intimidated and put the Hawks away with ease in Game One, 97–89.

Kyrie Irving was limited to 27 minutes, as his foot and knee were still giving him problems. The pain was so intense that the Cavaliers' coaching and training staff later decided to sit Kyrie out for the next two games. With Irving out, the Cavs needed someone to step up, and that someone ended up being J. R. Smith, who played the game of his life. Smith scored 28 points while nailing eight three-pointers in an incredible shooting display.

LeBron James could also not be stopped in the Game One victory, scoring 31 points to go along with six rebounds and six assists. Thompson had another double-double performance with 14 points and 10 rebounds. Timofey Mozgov had one, as well, with 10 points and 11 rebounds. The Atlanta Hawks may have been the higher seed, but after Game One, it was apparent that the Cavaliers were the favorites.

Cleveland was on a roll and it continued in Game Two, as they came out and crushed the Hawks in blowout fashion. Even without Irving, they were too much for the Hawks to handle, rolling to a 94–82 victory. LeBron again came within just one rebound of a triple-double, with 30 points, 11 assists, and nine boards. Thompson led all players in rebounds with 16 big ones.

Game Three in Cleveland would be a dogfight. The Cavaliers led throughout the game until a late run by the Hawks forced the game into overtime at 104–104. LeBron James and the Cavaliers rose to the occasion and put the Hawks away in overtime, 114–111, to take a commanding 3–0 lead in the series. Jeff Teague put up 30 points for the Hawks, but it wasn't enough to overcome Cleveland's total team effort. One point of note was that the scrappy play of Matthew Dellavedova got Hawks star center Al Horford so riled up, it caused him to elbow drop a downed Dellavedova and get himself tossed out from the game in the second quarter. The Hawks would later go on to call Dellavedova a dirty player, although they couldn't have been further from the case. They were simply bitter that they were getting beaten by the Love- and Irving-less Cavaliers.

LeBron James collapsed to the floor in exhaustion after the final buzzer went off. He played one of the best games of his life with a 37 point, 18 rebound, 13 assist triple-double performance for the ages. It truly was a total team effort, as Dellavedova scored 17 points, as did J. R. Smith off the bench. Shumpert brought 15 points and seven rebounds to the victory party, as well.

Riding the momentum of six straight wins, Quicken Loans Arena in Cleveland was rocking, and Game Four was never close, with the Cavaliers bombarding the Hawks and sweeping the series with a 118–88 victory. It was a blowout from the opening tip, as the Hawks couldn't overcome the emotional lift given to the Cavaliers by the returning Kyrie Irving. It was a very risky move by David Blatt, since Irving had been asked to sit out games two and three to rest his leg. If the Cavaliers had lost those games, they may have never recovered, but winning both gave them them confidence as well as the rest Irving needed. The Hawks could not stop the well-rested Irving, who had 16 points, five assists, and four rebounds in 21 minutes of action. The series was over, and Cleveland was headed to the NBA Finals.

The 2015 NBA Finals between the Cleveland Cavaliers and the Golden State Warriors had all the makings of a classic. The Warriors were coached by former NBA player and general manager Steve Kerr, who was in his first year on the Warriors' bench. Kerr won five NBA championships with the Chicago Bulls and San Antonio Spurs. The man knew what it took to win and showed as much, leading the Warriors to an NBA-best 67 wins for a whopping .817 winning percentage.

The Warriors finished with one of the best regular seasons in NBA history, and the greatest in the team's sixty-nine-year existence. Kerr also led the Warriors to a 12–3 playoff record with a sweep over the New Orleans Pelicans in round one, a six-game series win over Memphis in round two, and a five-game series win against the high-powered Houston Rockets to reach the finals.

Golden State was led by league MVP and sharpshooter Stephen Curry, who finished the season with a 23.8 scoring average along with one of the best three-point shots in the game. His career average from beyond the arc was over 40 percent, and he was on his way to becoming one of the greatest shooters in NBA history. Curry's father, Dell, also played in the NBA with Cleveland, Toronto, Charlotte, Utah, and Milwaukee.

Curry is not the only son of a former player in the vaunted Warriors backcourt; his "Splash Brothers" teammate Klay Thompson is the son of former NBA player Mychal Thompson. He, too, had a great season, finishing with 21.7 points a game and shooting .418 for his career beyond the arc. They possessed the best backcourt in the NBA and presented a very tough test for the Cavs to try to cover, especially with Irving still banged up with the ankle and leg injuries. Mix in the threat of Harrison Barnes, the speedy small forward who was looking to torch the Cavs and show them how wrong they were to choose Dion Waiters over him in the 2012 NBA draft; and Draymond Green, who was set to defend LeBron James in the matchup of his life. Las Vegas had the Warriors as a 3–1 favorite.

It was a matchup of the Cavs' experience and poise over the Warriors' flash and youth. The Cavaliers were bigger, more athletic, and, most of all, battled-tested and ready to win big. The Warriors had faced little adversity all season, while Cleveland had faced nothing but adversity, as three of their original starters from opening night in Anderson Varejao, Kevin Love, and Kyrie Irving hadn't played for the majority of the playoffs. Varejao didn't even get that far, Love was hurt in the Boston series, and Irving had been banged up since the second-round matchup with Chicago.

Game One at Golden State was a classic, with both teams bringing their best. The Cavaliers held a 14-point lead early in the second quarter before the Warriors came back to tie it and take the lead. It came down to the end with the score knotted up at 98 apiece. Golden State had the ball with 26 seconds to go when Stephen Curry made a great move to blow past Kyrie Irving. It looked like a sure layup for Curry to win the game, before all of a sudden Irving stuffed Curry from behind in one of the greatest hustle plays in NBA Finals history. The Cavaliers recovered the loose ball and called timeout with 24 seconds left to set up a potential game-winning shot.

The final possession of regulation would later be greatly criticized and disputed when LeBron James merely dribbled the ball for 21 seconds before chucking up a shot with a hand in his face that didn't even come close to reaching the hoop. Iman Shumpert caught the rebound and heaved up one last desperation shot, but it rattled in and then out, sending the game into overtime.

The extra period belonged to the Warriors, as they scored the first 10 points and the Cavaliers went ice cold from the field. The Warriors would hold on to win, 108–100, to take Game One of the series. The loss was painful enough for Cleveland, because it was a game they could clearly have won. What was more painful was the fact that midway through overtime, Kyrie Irving clashed knees with Klay Thompson and fell to the floor in tremendous pain. Kyrie had to hobble off the court, and it was later revealed he had a fractured kneecap, causing him to need immediate surgery and miss the rest of the NBA Finals. It was a fatal blow for Cleveland.

Irving was having a great game before the injury, appearing healthy and rested on his way to 23 points, seven rebounds, and six assists. Tristan Thompson had yet another big game as he pulled down 15 more rebounds. LeBron James had one of this best NBA Finals games with 44 massive points, eight rebounds, and six assists. It was a shame his incredible performance was wasted in a losing effort. Knowing that they had played one of their best games with Irving, and still lost, was a bitter pill to swallow in a silent postgame locker room.

With their backs against the wall and the odds fully against them, the Cavs entered a must-win game early on in the series at the Oracle Arena in Oakland. It was another tight game that went right down to the wire. Matthew Dellavedova, starting in place of the injured Irving, played the defensive game of his life and shut down Stephen Curry (5 of 23 shooting) every time he guarded him.

LeBron James got mugged virtually every time he touched the ball, and the officials refused to call a foul. It was one of the worst-documented cases of officiating in NBA history. The league went back and reviewed the tape after the game and even admitted to countless mistakes made by the officials. Despite being tackled almost every time he touched the ball, LeBron and the Cavaliers still had a chance to win the game after blowing an 83–72 lead with only three minutes to go. It was tied 87 with seven seconds left. Curry had just hit a layup to tie the game, and the Cavaliers would once again have the last shot in regulation. Knowing full well the heavy backlash he received after not driving the lane for the final shot in Game One, LeBron didn't waste any time going straight to the hoop with this one. Sadly, he was once again clearly fouled but the officials chose not to call it, instead swallowing their whistle and allowing the game to reach overtime.

The first minute of overtime was scoreless, with both teams appearing tentative. Iman Shumpert broke the tie with a three-pointer from the corner off a beautiful pass from LeBron James to put the Cavaliers ahead, 90–87, with 3:47 to go. LeBron hit two foul shots thirty seconds later, and the Cavaliers led by five. The Warriors responded with six straight points to take a 93–92 lead with only 30 seconds left in overtime. It looked like the Cavaliers were about to suffer their second straight heartbreaking loss.

With 11 seconds to go, James Jones put up a three-pointer but missed it badly. Matthew Dellavedova dove for the loose ball on the ground and was fouled by Harrison Barnes in the process. With all the pressure on his shoulders, Dellavedova, the little-known backup point guard from Australia, became an NBA Finals hero when he calmly stepped to the line and knocked down both foul shots to give the Cavaliers a 94–93 lead.

With seven seconds left, Stephen Curry took a 19-foot jump shot that missed, and LeBron gathered the rebound and was quickly fouled with four seconds left. LeBron missed the first foul shot but hit the second one to put the Cavaliers up by two. The Warriors were without a timeout and had to travel the distance of the court. Curry made a bad pass that was stolen Shumpert, and it was game over. Against all odds, the Cavaliers had won, 95–93, and evened up the series, which was now headed to Cleveland for Game Three.

The NBA Finals returned to Cleveland for the first time since 2007, and Cavaliers fans filled Quicken Loans Arena ready, willing, and able to cheer their team on to victory. Unlike Game Three of the 2007 NBA Finals against the Spurs when their Cavaliers were down 2–0 against a dynasty, this time they held the momentum and truly believed their team could win it all.

Riding the momentum of a raucous crowd and the euphoria of playing in the NBA Finals on their home turf, the Cavaliers played inspired ball through the first three quarters of Game Three and held a 72–55 lead heading into the final quarter. Holding Golden State to only 55 points through three quarters was almost unheard of. Golden State was used to having scored that many points midway through the second quarter of most games, but the incredibly scrappy defense and heart shown by the Cavs continued to throw off the Warriors.

Everything would change in the fourth quarter, however, as the Warriors closed what was once a 20-point lead down to just three points at 94–91 with 19 seconds to go. Curry caught fire and hit everything in sight. He scored 17 fourth-quarter points on the strength of five three-pointers. He was red hot, but the Warriors were out of time as the Cavs managed to hang on and win, 96–91, after two LeBron James foul shots.

It was a blowout that turned into a nail-biter, but it didn't matter to the Cavaliers and their fans, who were just happy to have the 2–1 series edge. Stephen Curry scorched the Cavaliers for 27 points and seven three-pointers, but it simply wasn't enough to overcome the Cavaliers. His fellow Splash Brother, Klay Thompson, was held to only 14 points. Curry stated after the game that he had discovered the secret to beating the Cavaliers defense in the fourth quarter. He would need it if they were to have any chance at coming back in the series.

Matthew Dellavedova did it again, stepping up on the biggest of stages by scoring 20 clutch points for the Cavaliers. He added five rebounds and four assists in another Herculean effort. LeBron continued to amaze as only he could, with another outstanding effort against all odds. James scored 40 points with 12 rebounds and eight assists. Tristan Thompson contributed another double-double with 10 points and 13 rebounds.

Game Four would be pivotal after LeBron and the Cavaliers had pulled off a near miracle by winning two of the first three games and would need to continue their magic against steep odds. The Warriors had won a league-high 67 games, and it was only a matter of time before they just outmatched the Cavaliers, but the only question was, would it be too late?

Steve Kerr made a switch to his starting lineup for Game Four by removing Andrew Bogut, who had been shying away from playing aggressive, physical defense, instead opting to start the smaller but quicker Andre Iguodala at center. Kerr was well aware that the Cavaliers had been using a seven-man rotation with only James Jones and J. R. Smith getting substantial minutes off the bench. Kerr knew that if he inserted Iguodala and went with a smaller, quicker lineup, it would only be a matter of time before the tired Cavaliers team would run out of gas. Kerr told his team to run the ball down the court every time and cause as many fast breaks as possible. He knew the constant pressure and long rotation would eventually wear down the Cavaliers and force them into turnovers. Kerr was exactly right, and the Golden State Warriors blew Cleveland out by a score of 103–82.

Iguodala rewarded his coach's faith in him and used his speed and energy to run circles around the Cavaliers' tired defenders all night long. He finished with 22 points and eight rebounds in 39 minutes, including four three-pointers. He also did an excellent job covering LeBron James and limited the Cavaliers' best player to just 20 points on 7 of 22 shooting. Iguodala was a nuisance for Cleveland to deal with the entire game.

His great play helped loosen the exhausted Cavaliers defense, allowing Stephen Curry to get wide open and nail shots. Curry had his best shooting game of the series, with 22 points on 8 of 17 shooting. Curry also picked up from where he left off in Game Three behind the line by hitting four three-pointers to keep the Cavaliers at bay.

Matthew Dellavedova looked like a shell of himself from Game Three, a game he played so hard in that he needed to check into the hospital the next day with dehydration. Apparently, he had been in the habit of drinking a 16-ounce coffee before each game, and then another eight ounces at halftime. Not the smartest of habits when playing on the biggest stage. Dellavedova was known for his great defense, so much so that it covered up for one of the weakest offensive skill sets in the NBA. The Cavaliers were able to get past Dellavedova's play on the offensive end because he usually made up for it on the defensive end, but on this night he didn't, and it killed them.

The blame for the Game Four loss could go to several people, but David Blatt's seven-man rotation was the glaring reason. He was playing his top five for far too long, and they were getting exhausted. His first two guys off the bench couldn't hit a shot, and it was over quickly. Blatt now had two days to prepare a better game plan for Game Five back in Oakland, as Steve Kerr had just outcoached him, and it was suddenly a three-game season where they couldn't afford any more mistakes.

The Cavaliers had a bench packed with solid veterans who were all loaded with playoff experience, some of them with NBA Finals experience. On his bench David Blatt had Kendrick Perkins, who had finals experience with Boston and Oklahoma City. Sitting there was Mike Miller, who had won a championship with LeBron James in Miami. James Jones was also on a championship team in Miami and had proven he could make several big shots when called upon. Shawn Marion was also no stranger to NBA playoff basketball. Cavaliers fans wondered what Blatt was waiting for, and would it be too little too late if he did start playing them? Those questions and more would need to be answered heading into the pivotal Game Five.

It was crystal clear that the Cavaliers were greatly undermanned heading into that game, with three of their starters from opening night gone. The depleted roster had defied the odds for four games and hung tough with the league's best team, based solely on the strong play of LeBron James, Tristan Thompson, and Timofey Mozgov.

In Game Four, Mozgov led the Cavaliers with 28 points while also pulling down 10 rebounds. He was one of the few bright spots in the game and series for the Cavaliers, and yet David Blatt chose to ignore this fact heading into Game Five. Mozgov started the game, but Blatt played him for less than five minutes before benching him for most of the rest of the game, only reinserting him once for a few minutes. It didn't make sense. Blatt would claim that he was trying to go small to match the speed of the Warriors, but it made no difference, as the Cavaliers fell, 104–91.

LeBron James, as great as he is, can't beat a team of five on his own, and that is exactly what the finals were shaping up to be. Some experts felt that the Cavaliers would have won the series in five games, if not outright swept the Warriors, with a healthy Irving and Love. The simple fact that the Cavaliers were able to keep it as close as they did was a near miracle in itself. There was also some talk that LeBron James, even if the Cavaliers didn't win, might still be awarded the Finals MVP trophy. His numbers through five games were among the greatest in NBA Finals history. He was averaging 36.6 points, 12.4 rebounds, and 8.8 assists a game, nearly a triple-double. Typically, if a player puts up numbers like that, his team is hoisting up the Larry O'Brien Trophy when it is over. This time, however, it was another case of not enough help for the greatest player on the planet, almost the exact same story as when he left Cleveland nearly five years earlier to the day.

It quickly became clear that that the Cavaliers would have a high mountain to climb in Game Six if they had any visions of saving the series when the visiting Warriors started the game on fire and built a 28–15 lead after one quarter. To their credit, they showed immense heart and didn't give up, cutting the lead to 45–43 at the half with an inspired second quarter of play.

The comeback proved to be nothing more than a mirage, as the Warriors regained the momentum in the third quarter by outscoring the Cavaliers, 28–18, to take a 12-point lead heading into what would become the final quarter of the NBA season. The lead ballooned to 94–79, giving Golden State their largest lead of the game, 15 points, with a little over four minutes to play. J. R. Smith, who had a subpar NBA Finals, finally woke up and starting hitting threes, making three of them in the final four minutes to help Cleveland make one last run, but it was too little too late, and the Golden State Warriors had won the NBA championship with a 105–97 victory.

LeBron James finished Game Six with 32 points, 18 rebounds, and nine assists, but with little to no help, it simply wasn't enough. Stephen Curry and Andre Iguodala led the Warriors with 25 points each, as both were left wide open for big baskets.

Late in the game, with the Cavaliers defense running on empty, both players drove the lane at ease to rack up their impressive point totals.

In a mild shocker of sorts, it was Andre Iguodala and not league MVP Stephen Curry who won the NBA Finals MVP award. Iguodala finished the series averaging 16.3 points a game with 5.8 rebounds and four assists. Curry had much better numbers with 26 points, 5.2 rebounds, and 6.3 assists a game. Regardless of who was named the MVP, the fact remained that Cleveland had once again fallen short. The hard work would soon begin for another shot the following season.

CHAPTER 2

Building a Champion

AT FIRST GLANCE, LEBRON JAMES had the series of his life, as he was the only viable scoring threat left on the Cleveland roster. He was the only player in NBA Finals history to lead both teams in scoring, rebounding, and assists, averaging 35.8 points, 13.3 rebounds, and 8.8 assists a game throughout the finals, a near triple-double. He even received several first place votes for the MVP award. The problem was that it wasn't too long after the finals were over that reports once again started circulating about his poor relationship with head coach David Blatt.

ABC had cameras in the huddles during timeouts, showing Blatt doing his best to motivate the team and work on strategy. However, LeBron was ignoring everything the coach had to say and oftentimes looked to be disengaged. Despite his tremendous play on the court, reports would quickly come out following the finals that confirmed James's direct disrespect of Blatt during timeouts.

Mike Tirico, who was the lead radio announcer for ESPN Radio along with Hubie Brown, was right next to the Cavaliers' bench during the finals and noticed what was going between Blatt and James. Appearing on the Matt Dery show on Detroit Sports 105.1 radio, Tirico gave his point of view that Blatt didn't do any coaching from the sidelines, and James's disrespect of him pretty much left the coach as nothing more than a glorified cheerleader just standing there.

ESPN beat reporter Marc Stein was able to second Tirico's point, since he was covering the series from the sidelines and noticed the same antics from James and other veterans. According to Stein, there were even times that Blatt would draw up a play during a timeout, only for James to reach over and erase the board and tell the team they were going to do something else.

With all of this going on, it wasn't a surprise when the ABC cameras cut to the Cavaliers' locker room at halftime and it appeared that players such as J. R. Smith weren't even paying attention but rather blatantly ignoring Blatt during his halftime speech trying to lift the spirits of his team and inspire them to come out in the second half and play better, saving the season. Smith had a checkered past when it came to respecting authority and wasn't a good influence on James to begin with.

Other problems became even more noticeable when it was later discovered that assistant coach Tyronn Lue had been calling timeouts from the sideline instead of the head coach. It was also leaked that Lue was hanging out with players on off days in social situations. What made this look particularly bad was the added factor that Lue was passed over for the head coaching job by Dan Gilbert in favor of Blatt before the season began. How often does a team put two people who competed for a job on the same staff, let alone not allow the head coach to pick his own assistants? Warts were starting to get uncovered.

Some of the biggest criticisms of LeBron James during his first stay in Cleveland were that he received preferential treatment and was never a mature player off the court. It appeared that he grew up during his four years in Miami, when the Heat and Pat Riley didn't cater to him the way the Cavaliers and Gilbert did. It wasn't too far into his return to Cleveland that LeBron starting soaking up the preferred treatment once again.

Even the staunchest LeBron James supporters couldn't ignore the fact that he was starting to fall into his old bad habits. One such case was after Game Four of the Chicago series when James didn't hesitate to tell reporters that he erased Blatt's final play and instead called his own play, overriding the coach. Albeit true, those are the types of things you keep in house and not make mention of to the media.

The other problem was that at the end of Game One in Golden State when the Cavaliers had the chance to win the game in regulation, it was James who dribbled the ball down to a few seconds left on the clock before chucking up a fall-away shot that had little to no chance of going in. No one heard James running his mouth after that missed shot that he overrode the coach to call that play when it was clear that he did.

James continued to hurt his chances at redemption later in the series. After the Game Five loss that put the Cavaliers behind, 3–2, he was asked about the outcome of the series and if he was worried. James responded, "I'm the best player in the world." It was uncalled for and something the greatest players of all time such as Michael Jordan didn't even have to say. It was a shame because every time it appeared that LeBron was finally getting it, he would do or say something selfish and stupid and once again get everyone to question his leadership skills.

Earlier in the season when Kevin Love was going through a tough patch, James publically, but very passive-aggressively, called out Love on Twitter to start fitting in instead of approaching Love in the locker room, in private, man to man. These actions and behaviors are not becoming of a leader, and it continued to tarnish what should have been a spotless career for James.

General manager David Griffin called an emergency press conference two days after the finals to address plans for the off-season and also squash the rumors of locker room unrest between his coach and superstar. The media in attendance wasn't buying it and continued to hammer Griffin, along with Blatt, who was also there with questions about his relationship with LeBron and very questionable rotations during the Finals after the Kyrie Irving injury. Other questions included the benching of Mozgov in Game Five and the decision to not play Kendrick Perkins, Joe Harris, and Mike Miller much in the finals. Shawn Marion never even touched the court and retired following the season.

Blatt did a great job of pretending nothing was wrong, but the questions just kept coming and the press conference became very awkward. He was in a no-win situation at times. If Blatt stood up to James, he was liable to get fired if the superstar pulled his weight. This had happened early in the 1981–82 season with the Los Angeles Lakers when superstar Magic Johnson couldn't get along with head coach Paul Westhead. Johnson demanded a trade knowing that owner Jerry Buss would eventually cave to the superstar and fire Westhead, which is exactly what occurred. Blatt knew he was on thin ice and had to choose his words carefully. It would only be a matter of time.

At the same time, however, he looked like a coward and less of a coach for not standing up to his superstar and taking the reins of the team. Blatt had horrible relations with the media all year. Every time he was questioned about a move, he would quickly become defensive and remind the reporters that he coached overseas for thirty years and was not a rookie. Blatt did not come off well by doing this, and, coupled with his handling of the LeBron James issue, both fans and media lost respect for him.

Tyronn Lue was the man Blatt beat out for the job, so it came as a surprise that he was named as one of the assistant coaches. Lue was a former professional player who was selected 23rd overall by the Denver Nuggets in the 1998 draft and traded to the Los Angeles Lakers with Tony Battie in exchange for Nick Van Exel on draft night. Lue will forever be remembered as the man who shut down Philadelphia superstar Allen Iverson in the 2001 NBA Finals, which the Lakers won in five games. It was the highlight of his playing career. He went on to spend time with the Washington Wizards, Orlando Magic, Houston Rockets, Atlanta Hawks, Dallas Mavericks, and Milwaukee Bucks, once again returning to the NBA Finals in 2009 with the Orlando Magic.

Known as a smart player and a leader on the floor, it was no surprise when he was named director of basketball development for the Boston Celtics at the start of the 2009–10 regular season. He performed well in that role before leaving in 2013 to join the coaching staff of the Los Angeles Clippers. He joined the Cavaliers a year later, becoming the highest-paid assistant coach in the NBA after being beaten out by Blatt for the head coaching job. It was a move that would prove to have gigantic repercussions only a short while later.

Lue was not the only former player Blatt chose to have on his staff; he also brought in former Cavalier Vitaly Potapenko. Selected 12th overall by the Cavaliers in the 1996 draft, he never reached his full potential at power forward and center, and would bounce around the NBA, also playing for the Boston Celtics, Seattle SuperSonics, and Sacramento Kings before retiring following the 2007 season. His coaching résumé had the Indiana Pacers on it, as well as the Fort Wayne Mad Ants, Dakota Warriors, and Santa Cruz Warriors of the NBA D-League. Potapenko would be counted on heavily to work with the big men on the Cavaliers' roster. Little did anyone know just how crucial the play of a big man would be to the team.

Aside from the Blatt-LeBron drama, the Cavaliers still needed to make sense of the roster, as all but a few of their players would be free agents or have the chance to opt out of their contracts and become free agents after the season. Players with one year left on their contract and who had the option to opt out were LeBron James, Kevin Love, J. R. Smith, and Mike Miller.

The restricted free agents—meaning that the players would have a chance to sign with another team, but Cleveland would have the option to match the money and keep the player—were Iman Shumpert, Matthew Delavedova, Timofey Mozgov, and Tristan Thompson. David Griffin would be smart to pay whatever was offered to Shumpert, because his defense was a big reason why the Cavaliers were able to go on their second-half surge. Shumpert had also showed heart playing hurt during the NBA Finals while doing an incredible job covering Klay Thompson.

Unrestricted free agents with the option to sign anywhere they wanted without the Cavaliers doing anything about it were James Jones and Kendrick Perkins. Locked up under contract with the Cavaliers were Kyrie Irving, Anderson Varejao, and Joe Harris. They also had Brendan Haywood under contract for one more season, as well, but with his 10.5 million-dollar salary not guaranteed, he was as good as cut.

James, Love, and Smith were all expected to opt out of their contracts with James and Love both expected to re-sign one year deals. The reason behind it was that both could earn maximum dollars by once again becoming free agents in the summer of 2016, when the NBA salary cap was raised. Smith was a different story: his play was hot and cold, and few knew if the Cavaliers would be willing to offer him large dollars to stick around. Mike Miller, despite a poor season, was good friends with James and would certainly pick up his option for one more year of sitting on the bench.

The million-dollar question was if free agent Tristan Thompson would re-sign with the Cavaliers or test the market. It was almost certain that his agent would demand a max contract, which he touted during his incredible run during the playoffs. The Cavaliers already had a starting power forward, and as long as Kevin Love was on the team, Thompson would have to come off the bench. Were the Cavaliers willing to pay top dollars to a backup? They were already paying injury-prone and seldom-healthy Anderson Varejao 30 million dollars.

Shawn Marion would be retiring, and the chance of under-achieving James Jones being re-signed was very slim. With only a few players under contract, the summer was about to get very interesting. The first step was to bring back the two biggest names, James and Love. The hope was that everyone would follow suit after that.

One thing they knew they didn't have to worry about was All-Star point guard Kyrie Irving returning, since he was already under contract for several more seasons. His health would be the only question. There was no doubt that Irving was not only one of the best players on the team and in the entire NBA, but his journey there was anything but ordinary.

Irving had basketball in his blood: his father, Drederick, played for Boston University and went on to play professional basketball in Australia for the Bulleen Boomers. Kyrie was born on March 23, 1992, in Melbourne, Australia, and his family would eventually relocate to the United States when he was two years old. He grew up around the game in West Orange, New Jersey, watching his dad play in various leagues.

Because of the death of his mother when he was four years old, and with his Dad on the road so much, he spent a lot of time with various aunts and uncles as he was growing up. There was no denying the hunger and skill that Irving had inside of him to succeed at basketball, and he played on several teams growing up to perfect his craft. Kyrie played for the Road Runners of the Amateur Athletic Union, more commonly known as AAU, a premier organization that many of today's top NBA stars played in growing up before and during their high school days.

Kyrie Irving was a star recruit when he entered Duke University from St. Patrick High School as a freshman. Duke was excited to land the coveted recruit, who was coming off a great high school career. Irving had played for Montclair Kimberley Academy in his freshman and sophomore years, where he averaged 26.5 points, 10.3 assists, 4.8 rebounds, and 3.6 steals a game. He became only the school's second 1,000-point scorer. He had his first taste of a high school championship in his sophomore year, when he led Montclair to its first New Jersey Prep B state title.

In a shocking move, Irving chose to leave Montclair for St. Patrick because he wanted to seek a bigger challenge at a school that would get him noticed by top universities such as Duke. The move to switch schools paid off for Irving: his game reached the next level his junior season when he averaged 17 points per game with five rebounds and six assists along with two steals per game. The team excelled with Irving in control, winning the New Jersey Tournament of Champions. The following year, they went 24–3 and won the Union County Tournament championship. Kyrie finished his high school career with an average of 24 points, five rebounds, and seven assists per game in his senior season.

It was while in high school, in the summer of 2009 between his junior and senior years, that he got his first real taste of international ball when he played in the Nike Global Challenge. He had earned his US citizenship years prior and was able to play.

It was a good thing for Team USA that he did, as he led them to the to the tournament title. Not only did he get his first gold medal, but he was the MVP of the tournament, averaging 21.3 points and 4.3 assists per game. Following his senior year, in June 2010, Irving was a part of the United States gold medal-winning team at the FIBA Americas Under-18 Championship.

Duke was getting one of the top prospects in the country, as the accolades for Irving were many. Irving was the MVP of the 2010 Jordan Brand Classic. He was ranked the number two player in the class of 2010 by Scout.com. He was also ranked the number three player in the ESPNU 100 and rated as the fourth-best player overall by Rivals.com. ESPNU also showed the young star some serious love when they ranked him the best point guard in the nation coming out of high school.

As a freshman, he was leading the Duke Blue Devils in scoring at 17.4 points per game on 53.2 percent shooting through the first eight games of the season. He didn't just excel at scoring, but he added 5.1 assists, 3.8 rebounds, and 1.5 steals per game. The problem was that he only played eight games before he suffered a severe ligament injury in his right big toe that sidelined him for the remainder of the regular season. He was able to return for the NCAA tournament in March, helping Duke reach the Sweet 16 round of play, where they lost to Arizona, although Irving exploded for 28 points in the contest. The only thing keeping him from being a sure thing with the number one pick was his recent injury. Teams would be sure to look past that later in the round, but was he worth the first overall pick? It would be up to Cleveland to decide. Derrick Williams of Arizona was the other hot college prospect many in the national media saw possibly skipping past Irving for the number one overall selection.

The Cavs selected Kyrie with the first overall pick in the June 2011 draft and had huge hopes for him to lead the Cavaliers for many years to come. In his first chance to showcase his talents in front of a national audience at the 2012 Rising Stars Challenge, he didn't disappoint. Irving scored 34 points in the game and earned MVP honors.

In their first season with Kyrie, Cleveland finished 21–45 in a strike-shortened season. Irving won the 2012 NBA Rookie of the Year Award, receiving 117 of a possible 120 first-place votes. He was also selected to the NBA All-Rookie First Team. He averaged 18.5 points with 5.4 assists. These were impressive numbers for the rookie. The numbers could have been even better, but he missed 15 games due to injury. Once again, an injury kept Irving from reaching his full potential. Sadly, this was something that would become a familiar trait early in his career.

Expectations were high for Irving heading into the 2012–13 season. The injury bug bit him again, however, and he missed 23 games. He was injured in the summer league when he sustained a broken right hand after reportedly slapping it against a padded wall after committing a turnover. He managed to come back and start the season with the team until he injured his index finger in a loss to the Dallas Mavericks, forcing him to miss the next three weeks of action. It was his third injury in just a year and a half of professional play, and also his fourth in three seasons going back to his season at Duke.

He bounced back from injury and was still impressive enough to be voted to the Eastern Conference All-Star team. He had a great All-Star weekend, including winning the Three-Point Shootout championship trophy. He was also setting milestones very early in his career, which allowed fans to look past the early injury issues, like when he scored his 41 points against the New York Knicks. He became the youngest player in NBA history to score 40 points at Madison Square Garden. He achieved that while having to wear a face mask to protect his recently broken nose.

Irving led the team in scoring by averaging 22.5 points a game and also led the team in assists with 5.9 a game. It was clear to anyone who took the time to watch him play that he was quickly becoming one of the elite players in the NBA. The team's record didn't improve as much as he would have liked, which led to the firing of embattled head coach Byron Scott, who was replaced by Mike Brown.

Kyrie Irving was primed to have a breakout season as he entered his third year in the league, but once again injuries and lack of support hurt him and the team. Irving, however, continued to shine on the brightest of stages, winning the All-Star Game MVP award in New Orleans. He put on a show for the entire NBA and represented Cleveland extremely well in the process. He was locked in and led the Eastern Conference to a win with 31 points and 14 assists. He would finish the season with an average of 20.8 points, 6.1 assists, 3.6 rebounds, and 1.5 steals per game. He also set a career high with 44 points in a 96–94 overtime loss to the Charlotte Bobcats late in the season.

The most positive of all the signs for Irving heading into the 2014 offseason was that he only missed 11 games in 2013–14. While Cleveland was experiencing the joy and utopia of LeBron James deciding to return home, Irving was overseas once again perfecting his craft. He was a member of the USA basketball team in the 2014 FIBA Basketball World Cup. He led Team USA to the gold medal and was named tournament MVP. Early heat began between him and Derrick Rose, as he was chosen over Rose to start all nine games in the tournament at point guard. Rose was asked to come off the bench, since it was clear Irving had surpassed him as the premier point guard in the NBA and the world. It was the smart choice: Irving finished the tournament averaging

12.1 points and 3.6 assists per game. He saved his best for last and scored 26 points in the gold-medal game. This incredible effort led him to be named the 2014 USA Basketball Male Athlete of the Year.

With his popularity level through the roof due to his excellent play on the court, his endorsement stock began to rise, as well, when he took on the role of "Uncle Drew" in a series of Pepsi Max advertisements. It was a widely regarded and beloved campaign that also led to a massive amount of "Uncle Drew" bobble heads being created and sold at Cavs games and on eBay. His popularity also reached a new level when he was voted onto the cover of the NBA Live 14 video game.

Three years into his professional career, the accolades for Irving were aplenty, and if he could just stay healthy, he could be the top point guard in the NBA for a very long time to come. By the time LeBron decided to come home, Kyrie was a 2010 McDonald's All-American, a 2010 Nike Hoop Summit All-American, a 2010 Jordan Brand High School All-American, a 2010 First-Team Parade All-American, a 2012 Rising Stars Challenge MVP, a 2012 NBA Rookie of the Year, a 2012 NBA All-Rookie First Team, a two-time NBA All-Star, a 2013 Three-Point Shootout winner, a 2014 NBA All-Star Game MVP, a 2014 FIBA Basketball World Cup Gold Medal winner, and a 2014 FIBA Basketball World Cup MVP.

Kyrie got off to a slow start finding the right chemistry with LeBron and Love in 2014-15 but eventually started to click and had another all-star season. Irving finished the regular season appearing in 75 games (a career high) and averaged 21.7 points and 5.2 assists a game. It was the lowest assist mark of his career, which was a bit concerning when you factor in that he had the most talent around him in the lineup. Cleveland fans and a lot of media still believe that if Irving had stayed healthy, the Cavaliers would have defeated the Warriors in the 2015 Finals. Irving was ruled unlikely to be ready for opening night of the 2015–16 season due to the left kneecap fracture he suffered in Game One of the 2015 NBA Finals, but the Cavaliers knew that once he came back, it would be well worth the wait.

The Cavaliers wasted no time bringing back the big Russian in the middle when they exercised the option to extend the term of Timofey Mozgov's contract on June 23 to include the 2015–16 season. It was a good early sign that the Cavaliers planned on bringing everyone back to make another run at the title. Mozgov was one of the lone bright spots in the NBA Finals, as he was one of the few members of the team to provide LeBron James with scoring support.

The 7'1" center came to the Cavaliers by way of a trade with the Denver Nuggets the previous January. Cleveland sent two protected 2015 first-round picks to Denver for Mozgov. He had pro sports in his blood: his father was a professional Soviet handball player.

Mozgov started playing pro basketball in Russia in 2004 with LenVo St. Petersburg, then played with CSK Samara and Khimki Moscow. Mozgov was also a member of the senior Russian national basketball team. He played at EuroBasket 2009, Eurobasket 2011, and the 2012 Summer Olympics. He played pro ball in Russia for six years before signing a three-year, $9.7 million contract with the New York Knicks in July 2010.

His time in New York proved to be short, as after only 34 games, he was traded to the Nuggets in a three-way blockbuster deal, which also involved the Minnesota Timberwolves and which brought Carmelo Anthony to New York. When the league went on strike the following season, he joined Khimki Moscow Region to stay sharp while everyone else were resting. He ended up spending parts of five seasons in Denver.

After losing Anderson Varejao to injury, The Cavaliers were desperate to find a big man who could start and play a large amount of minutes each game. Blatt had coached Mozgov on the Russian National team in 2012 that captured a bronze medal and knew exactly how physical he could be. It turned out to be the biggest pick up of the season, as Mozgov came up big for the Cavaliers. He started 45 games the rest of the season and averaged 10.6 points, 6.9 rebounds, and more than a blocked shot per game. He was the perfect solution in the middle, and the team proved to be unstoppable with him. He formed a perfect one-two punch with LeBron James when it came to pick and rolls, because it seemed like they knew where each other was on the court at all times.

Once again, the national media wasted little time trying to create worry that Kevin Love would leave Cleveland and sign elsewhere. Reports had him going back to the West Coast, with a landing spot of either the Lakers or Portland Trail Blazers. ESPN and several other national media outlets refused to believe that anyone would actually stay in Cleveland when they had a chance to become a free agent. Despite Love saying numerous times during the season that he would re-sign with the Cavaliers, the drama was still intense.

Kevin Love had to deal with national reporters all year spreading rumors about whether he would opt out after the season and leave Cleveland. He constantly had to hear how all his good numbers came on a bad team in Minnesota and thus didn't mean anything. Not a day would go by that another story wouldn't break about how Love didn't fit in with the rest of the team and how he and LeBron didn't get along.

Love just kept showing up, ignoring the nonsense and playing well, averaging 16.4 points a game. He also finished with an average of 9.7 rebounds in 75 games. His defense was lacking at times, however.

Since he grew up in Oregon, many rumors had him going back to the left coast. Loyalty was important to him, and that started at a young age. He loved to play basketball and took every chance he could to work on his game. On many nights his parents, Karen and Stan (a former NBA player), could look out the back window and he see him working for hours in the yard on his jump shot. He enjoyed success in high school while playing for the Lake Oswego Lakers. In his sophomore season, he averaged 25.3 points, 15.4 rebounds, and 3.7 assists per game, leading the school to the 2005 state championship game, where they lost to Jesuit High School. It was a great experience for Love despite not winning it all because it taught him how to compete at a championship level and instilled a deeper hunger inside of him to one day reach the pinnacle.

His high school career was also his first wake-up call of how political and business-minded the world of sports can be at times as he got caught up in the middle of a controversy. He was a member of the Portland Elite Legends AAU team but was removed from the team in the middle of the season because he had chosen to participate in the Reebok ABCD Camp against other top recruits being scouted by colleges. It seemed like a simple issue, but sadly, Nike wouldn't budge, and he was asked to leave. It ended up working out for Love, however, as it gave him time to play for the Southern California All-Stars instead. The switch of teams and leagues paid off well when the team compiled an unprecedented 46–0 record. In the midst of the run, Love's game just kept improving, and he collected three separate MVP awards along the way.

Meanwhile, after the AAU season was done, it was back to high school, and he continued to step up his junior year, averaging 28 points, 16.1 rebounds, and 3.5 assists per game. The team built off of his success and rode the momentum of his excellent play, returning to the state championship game. Love was determined not to lose the title game again. He was a seasoned player now and had won on several levels, and used that experience in the championship game by scoring 24 points and pulling down nine rebounds. Lake Oswego was not to be denied and behind the strong play of Love took home the state title.

It was time for his senior season, and Love was out to show the nation exactly why he was the top recruit in the nation. He put up "video game numbers" by averaging 33.9 points, 17 rebounds, and four assists per game. Those totals are almost unheard of for a high school athlete. It made some in the national media compare him to LeBron James during his amazing high school run. His remarkable season also helped Lake Oswego reached their third straight trip to the state championship game. It was a rematch of the prior year's final against South Medford High School. South Medford was led by future NBA player Kyle Singler, and they were looking for revenge against Love and Lake Oswego for the prior year's loss. Love did everything he could to help his team win, but despite scoring 37 points it wasn't enough, and his team lost the championship game.

Kevin Love finished his high school career in 2007 with one state championship and two runner-up finishes. The awards for Love just kept coming, as he was named the Gatorade National Male Athlete of the Year. He was also a first-team Parade All-American and finished his high school career as the all-time leading scorer in Oregon boys' basketball history with 2,628 points.

As he headed into college, it was expected that Love would play for Oregon, his father's alma mater, but it was never a real option despite pressure from the school's fans and alumni. Love could have attended any college of his choosing, being one of the top recruits in the world. After some mild consideration and flirting with North Carolina, he landed at UCLA, one of the most revered college programs in the country. UCLA won ten NCAA championships in twelve seasons between 1964 and 1975, a mark that will never again be touched. The run was under legendary head coach John Wooden, who was still alive when Love chose UCLA, and one of the key reasons Love went there was that Wooden was still a presence on campus. Love regularly went to Wooden and UCLA legend Bill Walton for advice. Love was a student of the game and didn't waste any time surrounding himself with people who could help fill his passion and hunger for basketball knowledge and growth.

The smart money was that Love would have skipped college altogether if the new rule weren't in place that required all high school students to attend college for at least one season. He was going to make the most of his one year of college experience, however, and immediately took to his surroundings and got ready to compete for the 2007–08 NCAA season. UCLA alumnus and school Hall of Famer Walt Hazzard gave Love his permission to wear his number 42 that had been retired in 1996.

Despite spending only one season at UCLA, Love once again made the most of his opportunity, leading to the Bruins to the regular season Pac-10 conference championship as well as the conference tournament championship. His excellent play also earned him a nomination to the All Pac-10 tournament team. Not surprisingly, the Bruins excelled under his leadership and that of his talented teammate Russell Westbrook, as they earned a No. 1 seed in the 2008 NCAA Tournament. The Bruins reached the Final Four, where they lost to the Memphis Tigers.

His outstanding play netted him consensus first-team All-American, Pac-10 Player of the Year, All-Pac-10, and Pac-10 Freshman of the Year honors. He led the Bruins with 17.5 points and 10.6 rebounds per game, and racked up 23 double-doubles.

Shortly after the Final Four exit, Love and Westbrook announced they would be leaving UCLA and entering the NBA draft. It was a draft loaded with talent. The Chicago Bulls used the first overall pick to select Chicago native Derrick Rose from the University of Memphis. The move paid off for Chicago right away, as the point guard went on to win the NBA Rookie of the Year Award. The Miami Heat used the second pick to draft Michael Beasley from Kansas State University. The Minnesota Timberwolves used the third pick to draft O. J. Mayo from the University of Southern California but traded him to Sacramento in a deal for for Love, who was selected fifth overall after Westbrook went fourth to the Seattle SuperSonics, who were about to become the newly minted Oklahoma City Thunder.

Kevin Love joined a Minnesota team that was in a state of flux, having struggled for years. They had lost their star, Kevin Garnett, to Boston a year earlier, and hopes of a turnaround were pretty much lost unless Love could spearhead the rebuilding project for them. Love played very well in the 2008 NBA Summer League for Minnesota, where he led the league in rebounding.

The regular season got off to a rough start and forced Love to encounter losing for the first time in his playing career, as the Timberwolves lost 15 of their first 19 games. The horrible start led to the firing of head coach Randy Wittman, who had been head coach of the Cavaliers during their dark days just prior to LeBron James's arrival. The dismissal of Wittman turned out to be a blessing for Love, because he received the chance to play for Hall of Famer Kevin McHale, who was stepping into the head coaching role from his general manager position.

Under McHale, Kevin Love's game began to blossom immediately, and he finished the season ninth in the league in rebounding, which was good enough to be first among rookies. He was a presence on the boards and was also ranked third in total offensive rebounds, as well as being ranked first in the league in offensive rebound percentage, becoming the first rookie to lead the league since Hakeem Olajuwon in 1984–85. Love could be counted on to score double digits every game, as well as pull down ten-plus rebounds, leading all rookies with 29 double-doubles, a Timberwolves rookie record. His great first season as a pro allowed him to be named to the 2009 NBA All-Rookie Second Team, and he also finished sixth in Rookie of the Year voting.

The hype for his second professional season was quickly derailed when it was announced that McHale would not return to coach the Timberwolves for the 2009–10 season. It was tough enough that the close relationship he had with McHale would not continue, but what happened next was even worse for the budding superstar. In a preseason game on October 16, 2009, against the Chicago Bulls, Love broke the fourth metacarpal in his left hand by banging it against the elbow of teammate Oleksiy Pecherov. The injury caused him to miss the first eighteen games of the season. It was a freak injury, but not nearly as freaky as the one he would suffer several seasons later that took him out of the most important postseason of his life.

It didn't take fans and new head coach Kurt Rambis long to realize the importance Love brought to the team: without him the Timberwolves were the worst team in the league, going a horrendous 2–16. The season was dreadful, with one of the few highlights being Love's selection to play in the NBA All-Star Weekend Rookie Challenge. The team's woeful performance didn't stop Love from continuing his dominance on the boards, as he finished the season ranked as the NBA's best rebounder per 48 minutes with 18.4, a mark good enough to beat out Dwight Howard and Marcus Camby.

Love's relationship with Rambis became strained during his third season as a pro. Love was the team's best player, but Rambis was not giving him the amount of minutes a player of his stature should have been receiving. Nine games into the season, Love was averaging only 28 minutes per game, exceeding 30 minutes only twice.

He continued to excel despite the lack of playing time, and in a home game against the New York Knicks on November 12,

2010, Love became only the nineteenth player to record a 30–30 game when he scored 31 points and pulled down a career-high 31 rebounds. His amazing rebounding total set a Timberwolves franchise record and was also the most by a player in an NBA game since Charles Barkley had 33 rebounds nearly 16 years earlier. He became the first player to have a 30–30 game since Moses Malone in 1982.

A little over a month later, on December 18, Love scored a career-high 43 points and had 17 rebounds in a 115–113 loss to the Denver Nuggets. The stellar performances earned Love a trip to play in his first All-Star Game later that season. The Timberwolves were a horrible 11–37 at the time of the All Star selection; otherwise, Love might have been a serious MVP candidate, averaging 21.4 points per game, with a league-best 15.5 rebounds, while shooting 43.9 percent from three-point range. He was also riding a streak of having 34 straight double-doubles.

Love remained hot following the break. On February 8, he would set a team record with his 38th consecutive double-double after scoring 20 points and recording 14 rebounds in the Timberwolves' 112–108 win over the Houston Rockets. It seemed every time Minnesota fans turned around, Love was breaking another team record. The trend continued on February 27 in a 126–123 win over the Golden State Warriors, when he scored 37 points and had 23 rebounds. It was his fourth 30-point, 20-rebound game of the season, but it was what he did at the free throw line that really made a mark. Love went 18 for 23 from the free throw line to tie Minnesota's team record for made and attempted free throws. His streak of games with double-digit rebounds and double-digit points finally ended late in the season, but not before he ran the streak to 53 straight games. It was the longest streak since the ABA–NBA merger in 1976, surpassing Moses Malone's 51-game streak from 1979 to 1980.

The incredible mark was just two short of Elvin Hayes's streak of 55 consecutive double-doubles set in the 1973–74 season.

It was no surprise that Love led the NBA in rebounding with an average of 15.2 per game. He was a runaway winner for the NBA Most Improved Player Award. He became the first player to average at least 20 points and 15 rebounds in a season since Malone in 1982–83. He finished the season with career highs in rebounding, scoring, assists, double-doubles, field goal percentage, free-throw shooting, three-point shooting, and minutes played. Because of his hustle on the boards and ability to score, he was clearly a fan favorite, as his No. 42 was the Wolves' top-selling jersey.

Kevin Love's attitude and ability were a huge positive for the Timberwolves, but their management refused to sign off on a long-term deal with him. After some heated moments and immense tension between the two sides, an agreement was finally reached when Love signed a deal to stay. It was for four years with a player option for Love to opt out after the third year worth up to $62 million. With the contract issues behind him, he began the following season where he left off, as he began by recording 15 straight double-doubles, the first player to do so since Hakeem Olajuwon at the beginning of the 1992-93 season. Love also continued to show his leadership ability and willingness to take the big shot when he made a three-point buzzer beater to defeat the Los Angeles Clippers on January 20, 2012. Love showed that he had nerves of steel and wasn't about to shy away from stepping up at crunch time.

Love earned a trip back to the All Star Game that season and won the Three-Point Shootout over Kevin Durant. It was remarkable to see a player of Love's size have such a naturally fluid outside shot. Seeing him rain down threes with the greatest of ease was a thing of beauty. The regular-season records just kept piling up for him, as well, when he set a franchise record for most games scoring 30 points or more in a season (19). He had a career-high 51 points in a 149–140 double-overtime loss to the Oklahoma City Thunder, as he continued to play his best against the league's top teams. Even with Love playing at his best, the Timberwolves couldn't get on track and finished with the Western Conference's fourth-worst record at 26–40. He was getting unfairly saddled with the reputation of being a great player on a lousy team, as he was named to the All-NBA Second Team and finished sixth in MVP voting. However, it was true; no matter how stellar he played, it didn't help the team win. It wasn't his fault, but he continued to take blame for it.

Following the season, Love was a member of the United States men's national basketball team that won the gold medal at the 2012 Olympics. It was on that team that he shared a lot of court time with LeBron James, and they meshed well. They helped the team finish undefeated, winning the gold medal over runner-up Spain.

The following season would once again start off with injury when Love broke the third and fourth metacarpals on his right (shooting) hand during a morning workout. Worried about being cast as injury-prone, Love worked his tail off and battled back quicker than anyone saw coming. He was expected to miss six to eight weeks but returned to the team in top shape just five weeks later. He didn't miss a beat, scoring 34 points while grabbing 14 rebounds in 35 minutes his first night back against the Denver Nuggets. The good karma wouldn't last long, however, as Love reinjured his shooting hand on January 3, 2013, at Denver and would miss another eight weeks.

Kevin Love was off to a great start when he was healthy enough to stay on the court, but injury concerns and a contract that was up in two years left several questions about his future heading into the 2013–14 season. Amidst trade talk and his unwillingness to sign with the Timberwolves long term, he continued to play well and not let the situation get to him. That year, he became the first player in NBA history to record 2,000 points, 900 rebounds, and 100 three-pointers in a single season. He also set the Timberwolves' franchise record for three-pointers in a season with 190. He was named to the All-NBA Second Team for the second time in his career.

Love played well in his first season after being traded to the Cavaliers. The lone concern was if he would be a one-year rental or a franchise player. As for Andrew Wiggins, the player traded away for Kevin Love, he gave the fans of Minnesota a glimpse at what they will be cheering for many years to come. Wiggins won the NBA Rookie of the Year award, averaging 16.9 points. Early signs point to Wiggins being a superstar in this league very soon.

Love would add to the drama when he opted out of the final year of his contract, worth $16.7 million in 2015–16, to become a free agent on June 24, 2015. The panic among Cavaliers fans didn't last too long: shortly after he became a free agent, he was spotted at a pool having a meeting with LeBron James. On July 1, 2015, Love re-signed with the Cavaliers on a multiyear maximum deal to keep him in Cleveland for a long time to come.

It was the first day free agents could sign with teams, and Love didn't waste any time. In LeBron James fashion, he made the announcement via a letter titled "Unfinished Business" on *The Players' Tribune*, a website where he is a senior editor.

In the letter, he wrote that, "Yeah, of course I've heard the free agency rumors. But at the end of the day, and after meeting with my teammates (it turns out pools are great meeting places) and with the front office, it was clear Cleveland was the place for me. We're all on the same page and we're all in. We have unfinished business and now it's time to get back to work."

With Love returning, it all but assured the fans and team that LeBron James would come back, as well, despite his announcing that he would opt out of his contract with the Cavaliers on June 28. Again, even as the national media did their best to make something more of it then it actually was, James quelled the worry and speculation quickly on July 10, when he re-signed with the team on another two-year contract with a player option for the second year.

James signed a deal he could once again opt out of after one year, because the salary cap was set to expand after the 2016 season and he knew he could make the most money by signing a maximum deal. He also knew that if for any reason the Cavaliers failed to win the championship in his second year back, another opt-out could force Gilbert and Griffith to fire Blatt.

The Big Three were set to come back for another run. Irving wouldn't be able to work out over the summer and would probably have to miss the early part of the season, but it didn't matter because their top three players were under contract. Two of them, Love and Irving, were locked up long term. Love's new contract also allowed fans who had been worrying that the Cavaliers gave up budding superstar Andrew Wiggins to simply rent Love for one season to take a deep breath.

July 1 was also a magical day for Iman Shumpert, as he agreed to return to the Cavaliers on a four-year, 40 million-dollar deal. He was a key ingredient on defense, helping shut down some of the best three-point-shooting attacks in the league. Shumpert was a great addition on the offensive side of the ball, as well, playing in 38 games and averaging 7.2 points off the bench. He also averaged 1.3 steals a game.

Like most of the Cavaliers, his rise to becoming one of the elite players in the NBA was never a foregone conclusion, as it was riddled with ups and downs along the way. Iman Shumpert's love of basketball started at a young age, and his talent grew every time his feet touched the court. As early as junior high, he showed he might have the talent to turn pro one day. Shumpert played at Gwendolyn Brooks Middle School in Oak Park, Illinois, where he played alongside Evan Turner, another future NBA player. His talent continued to grow while he played for Oak Park and River Forest High School. He excelled there as a First-Team All-State player and one of the country's top 30 seniors. The nation took notice when he was named conference MVP as a junior and senior and rated No. 15 among senior players by Scout.com and No. 26 by Rivals.com. He played in the 2008 McDonald's All-American Game and was named a Third-Team Parade All-American.

He attended college at Georgia Tech, where, in his junior season, he led his team in scoring (17.3 points per game), rebounding (5.9), and assists (3.5), becoming only the seventh player in ACC history to do so. He ranked fourth in the ACC in scoring, 15th in rebounds, 10th in both field goal and free throw percentage, and first in steals. His defensive skills were what really caught the eyes of pro scouts, and he was voted to the All-ACC Second Team and the conference's all-defensive team. With his junior season going as well as it did, he declared for the NBA draft, foregoing his final year of college eligibility.

The decision to skip college was a smart one for Shumpert: he was drafted with the 17th overall pick in the 2011 NBA draft by the New York Knicks. He was known for his on-the-ball defending and was quickly seen as one of the best defenders in the league. His first season would end with disappointment as Shumpert suffered a knee injury during a first round playoff game against the Miami Heat. An MRI revealed that Shumpert tore the ACL and meniscus in his left knee and would miss the rest of the series.

Overall, his rookie season was a success, as he finished fifth in the 2012 NBA Rookie of the Year voting. Shumpert was also the only rookie to receive votes for the Defensive Player of the Year award. He averaged 9.5 points a game with 2.8 assists, 3.2 rebounds, and 1.7 steals. Still recovering from surgery, he wasn't able to make his sophomore season debut until January 17, 2013, in a game against the Detroit Pistons at The O2 Arena in London. Because of the injury, all of his stats decreased in his second season. His numbers in 2013–2014 also remained about the same, as he failed to improve.

The 2014–15 season got under way on a high note for Shumpert and the Knicks when they beat the highly-favored, re-tooled Cavs squad in Cleveland's opener. After that victory, there wasn't much for the Knicks fans to get excited about, because they had one the league's worst records. On December 12, 2014, Shumpert dislocated his left shoulder in the second quarter of the Knicks' 101–95 win over the Boston Celtics and was subsequently ruled out for three weeks.

It would take longer for him to recover, however, and by the time Shumpert reached the Cavaliers on January 5 via a trade, he was still hurt and not playing. The Cavaliers knew of the defensive integrity that Shumpert brought with him and were willing to wait it out.

The Cavaliers were one of the worst perimeter-defending teams in the league, and they would count heavily on a healthy Shumpert to help in that department. He would eventually make his debut with the Cavaliers on January 23, 2015, and give them the perimeter defense they sorely needed.

Combined with the deal struck with Kevin Love and another rumored deal the team had with Tristan Thompson, adding Shumpert's contract meant the Cavs were approaching $240 million in new salary commitments on just the first day of free agency.

There was only one problem. The expectation that Tristan Thompson would come back right away as part of the package didn't materialize despite numerous reports that the two sides were about to ink a deal. It would take some time before that would become a reality, since Thompson believed he deserved a maximum contract himself, despite the fact that no other team offered him one. It would turn into a drama spanning many months, with the Cavaliers holding firm to their five-year, 80 million-dollar offer. It wasn't enough for the Canadian native, who insisted he wanted 94 million.

Thompson played well coming off the bench and adjusted to the role, finishing the 2014-2015 season averaging 8.5 points and eight rebounds a game. Despite his lack of playing time compared to past seasons, Thompson was able to retain most of the same numbers he had as a starter, including being the only Cavalier to play in all 82 games. Thompson would become a major factor in the playoffs as one of the sole squaring and rebounding threats next to LeBron James down the stretch.

Perhaps the biggest problem for Thompson was that he saw the contracts being handed out to other free agent forwards and his eyes and pockets suddenly got big. Kevin Love received a five-year deal worth $110 million. Marc Gasol also received a five-year deal for the same amount. LaMarcus Aldridge, a man considered one of the very top free agents, signed a four-year, $80 million contract with the San Antonio Spurs. As Thompson waited for the Cavaliers to pony up the extra 14 million, other players continued to sign massive deals. Enes Kanter, four years, $70 million; Greg Monroe, three years, $50 million; DeAndre Jordan, four years, $88 million; Draymond Green, five years, $85 million; Brook Lopez, three years, $60 million; and several others.

The longer it went on, the more unique the situation became, as several factors were at play. Thompson was a restricted free agent, and the Cavs had his Bird rights. This meant that they could offer him any amount without exceeding the salary cap (the cap exception was named for former Boston Celtics star Larry Bird, the first player signed under the rule). But, as a team, the Cavs were well over the salary cap. So if Thompson were to leave, they couldn't spend $80 million to find a replacement. They'd be left with only league-mandated exceptions to find cheap veterans as replacements. It was a heavy roll of the dice for the Cavaliers.

If Thompson chose to take the qualifying offer worth $6.8 million over one year, he'd re-enter free agency in the summer of 2016 as an unrestricted free agent, meaning he'd be in complete control over his future. However, it would be a giant risk for him, as well, because if he got injured or had an off year, his stock and worth could plummet. Making things even dicier was the fact that Thompson shared the same agent as LeBron James. When the roster was depleted, and they had no one to turn to, Thompson was one of the few players to step up. It was a loyalty factor in many ways that kept the Cavaliers from letting him walk.

Tristan Thompson was far from a franchise player, but he was one of the few that had grown up with Cleveland, and it made things even more emotional and dramatic. Until this point he had underachieved after being selected fourth overall in the 2011 NBA draft. Much like Irving, who was born in Australia, Thompson was born outside of the United States, in Toronto, Ontario, Canada, and raised in Brampton. Thompson was a physical power forward, standing 6'9" and weighing in at 238 pounds. He was the presence down low that the Cavaliers sorely needed.

He had a decent rookie year, was voted to the NBA All-Rookie Second Team. Thompson came off the bench behind veteran forwards Antawn Jamison and Anderson Varejao for the first three months of his rookie season but still managed to make his presence known on both ends of the court. His production increased in February as his minutes increased, and he recorded three double-doubles that month.

Expectations remained high for Thompson the following year, as they would for any top five pick. He could be counted on for double-digit rebounds and points per game but never was able to show what it took to take over the game. Despite his massive size, one of the biggest problems Thompson was faced with was getting his own shots blocked. Almost 17 percent of his shots were blocked, which was unheard of for a man of his size.

Where he did excel was on the offensive boards: he averaged 3.7 offensive rebounds per game, which ranked fifth in the NBA and first among second-year players. Another bright spot was when he set the Cavaliers franchise record for most offensive rebounds in a single season with 306, good enough to finish second in the NBA and to surpass Zydrunas Ilgauskas's 299 offensive rebounds in 2004–05. He collected a team-high 31 double-doubles on the season, becoming just the ninth player in franchise history to total at least 30 double-doubles in a single season. While injuries seemed to hamper Irving, they never did Thompson, who started all 82 games in the 2012–13 season and averaged 11.7 points with 9.4 rebounds and 0.9 blocks per game.

He continued to pull down rebounds in the 2013–14 season, racking up career-best 36 double-doubles, which was good enough to finish fifth in the Eastern Conference in that category. As good as he was on the boards, he still struggled with his shooting, so he decided to switch to shooting right-handed. It did help his foul shooting, as he improved to 69 percent, which is below average but still better than the 61 percent he finished with the prior season. He once again proved his durability by starting and playing in all 82 games.

Like his teammate Irving, Thompson was also a competitor on the international level. Thompson represented Canada Basketball at the FIBA Americas U18 Championship in 2008, where they won the bronze medal. He also competed at the 2009 FIBA Under-19 World Championship in Auckland, New Zealand.

Perhaps one of the biggest reasons for the Cavs to bring Thompson back was that, with the sole exception of Timofey Mozgov, they were short on big men whom they knew they could keep healthy. The fans and teammates loved Anderson Varejao, but he could not stay healthy.

Known as "Wild Thing" due to his unruly hairstyle and hustling play, Anderson Varejao was one of the most popular, and injury-prone, players in Cleveland Cavaliers history. He was born in Brazil and won a gold medal playing with Brazil at the 2003 Pan American Games. Prior to that, Varejao had played for Franca Basquetebol Clube in the city of Franca, São Paulo. He also spent time with with FC Barcelona Bàsquet of the Liga ACB before coming to the NBA in 2004, when he was selected 30th overall by the Orlando Magic.

His stay with the Magic was short: less than a month after he was drafted, Orlando traded him along with Drew Gooden and Steven Hunter to the Cleveland Cavaliers in exchange for Tony Battie and two future second-round picks. He was the only player who played with LeBron James during his first stint in Cleveland who was on the team at the time of his return. As a rookie with the Cavaliers, he caught the eye of fans with his energetic play and rebounding ability. He was a spark off the bench. He missed the first 32 games of the 2005–06 season with a dislocated right shoulder, as his high energy and intense play often led to injuries.

Varejao was a key off the bench in the Cavaliers' 2007 run to the NBA Finals. Despite his popularity being at an all-time high with fans because of his appearance and exciting play, it still didn't prevent Anderson from becoming a restricted free agent, and he did not sign a contract with the Cavaliers at the start of the 2007–08 NBA season. He was quick to remind the fans and team that this was also a business. His holdout was not short, and he didn't return to the Cavaliers until December 5, 2007, after he signed a two-year $11.1 million offer sheet with a player option for a third year at $6.2 million with the Charlotte Bobcats. Under the NBA's collective bargaining rules, the Cavaliers had one week to match the offer sheet given to Varejao and wasted no time doing so, signing him the very next day. Following the 2009 season, he refrained from going through the free agent drama again and signed a 6-year contract worth $42.5 million.

After LeBron James left the team after the 2009 season, it was crucial that Anderson step up his game as the new leader of the team. He didn't, partially because he was hit by the injury bug once again after playing in only 31 games. He suffered a torn tendon in his right ankle on January 6, 2011, and sat out the rest of the season. It was hard to get mad at Anderson for getting hurt so much, because you had to admire his aggressive play.

Heading into the 2011–12 season, the Cavaliers were hoping for Anderson to remain healthy and be a presence in the middle, but he only managed to play in 25 games. He suffered a broken right wrist on February 10, causing him to miss the rest of the season. At the time of the injury, he was averaging 10.8 points and 11.5 rebounds a game. It was more of the same from Anderson in 2012–13: his season ended not even halfway through the year when he was hospitalized for a blood clot in his lung. He had been averaging a career-best 14 rebounds a game. It was his third straight season playing 31 games or less.

In the 2013–14 season, his tenth in the NBA, Varejao started to get things back on track, becoming one of the focal points for an improving Cavaliers team. He played in 65 games, his most since 2009–10, averaging 9.7 rebounds and 8.4 points a game. Varejao was returning to form, and with Thompson playing power forward and

LeBron back to play small forward, Varejao could start at center or be the first big man option off the bench for coach Blatt. It was an exciting time to be a Cavalier, and Varejao had lived through it all. Sadly for Varejao, his 2014–15 season would end quickly because of injury. He only played in 26 games before tearing his Achilles tendon. It was just another reason why the Cavaliers needed to bring back Thompson despite the high price tag.

As the Cavaliers waited on Tristan Thompson to see what he would do, they continued to build a roster around their Big Three. Pressed into a starting role during The Finals, when Kyrie Irving was lost to injury after Game One, Matthew Dellavedova had some spectacular moments on the biggest stage, but it wasn't good enough to land him a major deal anywhere else, since he was seeking a multiyear contract worth four million dollars a year. To no one's surprise, not a single team was willing to offer Delly that kind of cash. Dellavedova's agent finally came to his senses and convinced his client to settle on a one-year deal to stay with the Cavaliers. The deal was worth approximately 1.2 million dollars for one season. Sure, his defensive skills could be game changing, but his offensive game was seen as one of the weakest in NBA history.

Mike Miller didn't waste any time recommitting to the Cavaliers, exercising his player option with the Cavaliers for the 2015–16 season on June 30, 2015. But the Cavaliers had different ideas for the aging forward, and on July 27, 2015, they traded him, along with Brendan Haywood and two future second-round draft picks, to the Portland Trail Blazers in exchange for cash considerations. Haywood carried a large contract with him and was the main focus of the deal. Fans and media worried that trading Miller away would upset LeBron James, but unlike during his first time in Cleveland, the Cavaliers brass continued to make bold moves without worrying about catering to the every whim of the superstar.

Sometimes when an athlete gambles on himself, it can pay off; other times, not so much. This was the case with J. R. Smith, who opted out of the final year of his $6.4 million contract with the Cavaliers to test the free-agent market. Smith initially opted out hoping that teams would be lining up to sign him for a long-term deal.

Sadly for Smith, he never received an offer. His disappearing act in the finals, combined with his immature antics off the court, scared teams away. He walked away from $6.4 million, and by the time he eventually resigned with the Cavaliers, he was forced to take a pay cut. On September 2, 2015, Smith re-signed with the Cavaliers for one year and a little over $2 million guaranteed with incentives and a player option, not exactly what he had planned.

Smith's journey in the NBA can only be classified as a mythical odyssey, with his attitude and off-court antics always seeming to get in the way of a great shooting touch. His life and career have been anything but simple; the man is an enigma. He grew up in Millstone, New Jersey, where he attended four different high schools. He started off at Steinert High School before transferring to McCorristin Catholic High School, then he transferred to Lakewood High School. It wasn't until he attended Lakewood that Smith played high school basketball for the first time. Things did not work out for him at Lakewood, either, so he then transferred to Saint Benedict's Preparatory School for his senior year and chose to play basketball there, as well.

It was hard for Smith to find any consistency in his game playing for so many schools and never really settling in anywhere. However, he did manage to average 27 points, six rebounds, and five assists in his senior season. He was also chosen as a Second-Team *Parade* All-American. That helped catch the attention of high-powered basketball colleges all over the nation, and he signed a letter of intent to play at the University of North Carolina.

After his 25-point performance at the McDonald's All-American Game in which he was named game co-MVP with Dwight Howard, Smith was convinced that he was good enough to play pro ball, and he decided to enter the NBA draft instead of college.

His risk to skip college paid off: he was taken 18th overall in the 2004 NBA draft by the New Orleans Hornets, and he performed well in his rookie season. Smith averaged 10.3 points, 2.0 rebounds, and 1.9 assists per game. He even showed a little bit of flair for the dramatic and spotlight when he decided to compete in the slam dunk competition during All-Star weekend. Despite being in a loaded draft class, Smith was named the Western Conference Rookie of the Month three consecutive times in January, February, and March. Even with the great play of their sharpshooting rookie, the Hornets did not improve and finished the season at 18–64.

His second season with the Hornets was a total mess across the board. Because of Hurricane Katrina, the Hornets spent part of the season in Oklahoma City. The moving around hurt Smith, and he slumped badly, averaging just 7.7 points, 2.0 rebounds, and 1.1 assists. Another key factor was that many of his shots were taken away by the incredible play of his rookie teammate Chris Paul. In fact, the great play of Paul would lead to a 20-game win improvement for the Hornets, who finished 38–44. After the season, the Hornets traded Smith and forward–center P. J. Brown to the Chicago Bulls for center Tyson Chandler. His time with Chicago lasted all but four days, as he was traded again, this time to the Denver Nuggets, for guard Howard Eisley and two 2007 second-round draft picks.

The move to Denver ended being the best thing to happen to him: the Nuggets were perennial playoff contenders with Chauncey Billups and Carmelo Anthony leading them. Smith got off to a rocky start with the Nuggets, however: only months into the season he was the centerpiece of a late-game brawl with the New York Knicks.

The incident took place with 1:15 remaining at Madison Square Garden. The Nuggets were ahead, 119–100, at the time. Denver had dominated most of the game and led by as many as 26 points at one point in the third quarter. The Knicks' Mardy Collins fouled Smith on a fast break by slapping his arms around Smith's neck, knocking him to the ground. Smith stood up to confront Collins, but Nate Robinson pushed Smith away and began shouting at him. Not one to opt for calmness, Smith charged into Robinson, who pushed back against him, causing both players to fall over photographers and into the front row of courtside seats. They would eventually be separated by teammates and officials before the mêlée could worsen. Just when it seemed like cooler heads would prevail, Carmelo Anthony punched Collins in the face, knocking him to the ground. This caused Jared Jeffries and Collins to chase Anthony as he retreated toward the Nuggets' bench, but they were restrained by teammates and coaches. In a shocking move, all ten players on the court at the time of the incident were ejected from the game.

The fallout of the brawl was massive, as seven players were suspended for a total of 47 games, and the players lost in excess of $1.2 million in salary. Each team was also fined $500,000. In his official statement, NBA commissioner David Stern stated, "It is our obligation to take the strongest possible steps to avoid such failures in the future." Anthony was suspended for 15 games and Smith for 10.

At the time of the brawl, Anthony was the league's leading scorer, and his suspension, along with losing Smith, caused the Nuggets to have to make a move. A day after Anthony was suspended, Denver acquired Allen Iverson, who was then second in the league in scoring behind Anthony. With the addition of

Iverson and the returning Smith, the Nuggets would have one of the best backcourts in the NBA. That trio led the Nuggets to 45 wins and the sixth seed in the Western Conference playoffs, where they lost to the eventual NBA champion San Antonio Spurs in the first round.

Smith finished his first season with the Nuggets averaging 13 points, 2.3 rebounds, and 1.4 assists. It wasn't a bad first year with the team despite missing 10 games for the brawl and suffering a torn meniscus in his left knee that required surgery, causing him to miss several weeks of playing time.

The playoff series against San Antonio was a completely different story for Smith, however, because it showed why coaches sometimes have a hard time trusting him in crucial situations. Smith, who was a 39 percent three-point shooter during the regular season, failed to connect on any three-point shots in the first four games and was criticized for poor decision making by coach George Karl. In a memorable press conference after Game Four, Karl informed reporters of his plan to bench Smith for Game Five. Karl said, "He's done," and explained his frustrations over Smith's poor judgment in shooting a three late in the game: "I have no idea what planet that came from." Karl told the Associated Press that he had drawn up the play to give the ball to either Allen Iverson or Carmelo Anthony. Karl continued, "And then, of course the one with eight seconds to go, from 50 feet, I just love the dignity of the game being insulted right in front of me." Karl was extremely angry at Smith, and he had every reason to be, as his team would go on to be eliminated by a superior San Antonio Spurs team.

Smith's second season with the Nuggets once again got off to a rocky start when he continued to show he couldn't be trusted to show maturity. On October 13, 2007, Smith was involved in an incident at a Denver nightclub. The Nuggets suspended him for the first three regular-season games of 2007–08 for his role in the incident. His numbers stayed steady but did not improve: he averaged 12.3 points, 2.1 rebounds, and 1.7 assists, and his team returned to the playoffs. He was determined to show that the previous playoffs were a fluke and that he could play with the best of them. In a four-game series in which his team got swept by the Lakers, Smith played well. He averaged 18.3 points per game on 53.5 percent shooting, with a three-point shooting percentage of 31.8 in the first-round sweep.

Smith's breakout season with the Nuggets was 2008–09. On April 13, 2009, Smith scored a career-high 45 points on 13 of 22 shooting, in a 118–98 home win over the Sacramento Kings. He made a franchise-record 11 three-pointers during the game, which was one shy of tying the NBA record. The Nuggets were also on a roll and made it to the Western Conference finals before getting beaten by the Los Angeles Lakers. Smith played well in the playoffs, going on to average 14.9 points per game on 45.4 percent shooting.

He carried the positive momentum with him the next season, finishing the 2009–10 season with averages of 15.4 points, 3.1 rebounds, and 2.4 assists. During the season, Smith scored 41 points against the Atlanta Hawks, which included 10 three-pointers, one shy of his record. The Nuggets, however, had another early exit from the NBA playoffs.

The start of the 2011 season saw a league-wide NBA lockout, due to a contract dispute between players and owners. While most players elected to stay home and rest up, Smith signed with the Zhejiang Golden Bulls of the Chinese Basketball Association. He made the most of his time in the foreign league by scoring 60 points off the bench during a 122–110 victory over the Qingdao Eagles in February. Also during his time with the Golden Bulls, Smith won a Foreign Player of the Week award and was selected as a starter for the Southern Division All-Stars in the 2012 CBA All-Star Game. He was having a great time in the league and pretty much had no choice but to stay there because he did not secure an opt-out clause, so he could not return to the NBA until the end of the 2011–12 CBA season. He eventually sued the Golden Bulls for one million dollars after the team withheld that amount from his salary claiming he missed many practices and faked an injury.

Smith was eager to get back to the NBA and signed with the New York Knicks just five days after his last game in Japan for $2.4 million. Smith was a solid pickup for the Knicks, who had been struggling most of the season with their three-point shooting. The Knicks greatly improved in that department because of Smith and the emergence of Steve Novak. Once again, his numbers remained steady, as he averaged 12.5 points, 3.9 rebounds, 2.4 assists, and a career-high 1.5 steals per game in 35 appearances for New York. The season would end in the first round of the playoffs when they took on the high-powered Big Three of the Miami Heat, losing in five games while Smith averaged 12.2 points but only shot 31.6 percent from the field and 17.9 percent from three-point range.

Despite his poor showing in the playoffs, the Knicks liked what they saw of Smith in their small sample, and on July 11, the Knicks and Smith agreed to a $2.8 million contract with a player option. On December 5, 2012, Smith hit the game-winning jump shot in a game against the Charlotte Bobcats as time expired for a 100–98 win. He would follow that up on December 26, 2012, when he connected on a shot with one second remaining that gave the Knicks, playing without Carmelo Anthony and Raymond Felton, a 99–97 victory over the Phoenix Suns. Smith was in the spotlight once again, and stepping it up.

So impressive was his play off the bench that he was awarded the NBA Sixth Man of the Year Award for the 2012–13 season. Many fans had compared him to past favorite John Starks, and this was further proof of that, because Smith was the first Knick to win the award since John Starks did it during the 1996–97 season. Smith set career highs in almost every category, averaging 18.1 points, 5.3 rebounds, 2.7 assists, and 1.3 steals in 33.5 minutes per game. He showed his durability by playing 80 games.

The New York Knicks entered the playoffs with their best regular-season performance since 1997, finishing atop the Atlantic Division for the first time since 1994. It was good enough to earn them the number two seed behind the Miami Heat. As good as the season was for Smith, he couldn't stay out of trouble when the playoffs came around and continued to make boneheaded decisions. This time it was when he was suspended for Game Four of the first round of the playoffs after elbowing the Celtics' Jason Terry in the chin. The Knicks would eventually get past Boston but lose to Miami in the second round.

Smith re-signed with the Knicks on July 11, 2013, for a reported $17.95 million over three years. The following season would be a nightmare, however, as only three days after signing his contract, Smith underwent surgery to repair a patellar tendon and a torn meniscus, both in his left knee. The problems continued for Smith when he was suspended five games on September 6, 2013, for violating the NBA's anti-drug program. Eventually, he would heal up from surgery and be able to rejoin the team, but things just kept going south for the once-promising star, and on January 8, 2014, Smith was fined $50,000 for unsportsmanlike conduct after repeated instances in which he attempted to untie the shoelaces of his opponents, causing him to lose the respect of his teammates, coaches, and fans.

His antics on and off the court didn't affect his confidence to shoot the ball, however. On April 6, 2014, Smith put up an NBA-record 22 three-point attempts in a 102–91 loss at Miami. He set a new team record with 10 made three-pointers, going 11-for-28 from the floor. He finished the spectacle by shooting 10-for-22 from beyond the arc with 10 attempts in the fourth quarter alone and ending up with 32 points. It was the lone bright spot of a miserable season in which the Knicks finished with one of the worst records in the league. The combination of injuries to their star players, off-the-court antics, and just the general chaos of the team kept them from achieving anything. A coaching switch would also be coming, with veteran player Derek Fisher eventually accepting the position in the offseason.

While his career on the hardwood was filled with ups and downs, his off-the-court life wasn't much more stable. On June 9, 2007, Smith and two passengers were injured in a car accident on Stagecoach Road in Millstone Township, New Jersey, when the SUV he was driving went through a stop sign and collided with another car. Smith and a passenger, Andre Bell, were ejected from the vehicle at around 5:30 p.m. Smith was taken to Jersey Shore University Hospital. Bell, a close friend of Smith's, suffered serious head injuries before being pronounced dead two nights later. Lucky enough for Smith, neither he nor the second passenger suffered life-threatening injuries. In October 2008, a grand jury in Monmouth County, New Jersey, declined to indict Smith on a vehicular manslaughter charge stemming from the accident. Smith's driving record included five suspensions in eight months.

Smith was not completely in the clear, however, and pled guilty to reckless driving two years later. Smith was initially sentenced to 90 days in a Monmouth County (New Jersey) jail, but 60 of those days were suspended, on the condition that he complete

500 hours of community service. On July 31, 2009, the *Denver Post* reported that Smith was released from jail after serving 24 days of his sentence. Smith totaled 27 points against his driving record from April 2005 to January 2006, including eight violations on seven different days, including five citations for speeding. This would be enough for most people to catch the hint and slow down, but since the accident, he has received two more speeding tickets and three license suspensions in New Jersey.

The NBA took notice of the incident and decided they needed to take action, and Smith was suspended for seven games on August 28, 2009, because of his guilty plea. Smith's legal problems weren't limited to cars. In May of 2012, he was arrested in Miami Beach, Florida, for failing to appear in court after he was cited for operating a motor scooter without a valid license.

It wasn't just on the court, or in the car, that Smith seemed to be getting into trouble; the world of social media got him in trouble, as well, via Twitter, when Smith closed his Twitter account (jr_smith1) on August 5, 2009, after he was accused of writing in a way that reflected the Bloods gang, specifically replacing his c's with k's. He would eventually reopen the account to post bare pictures of his posterior.

The Cavaliers looked past all of this when they made the trade on January 5, 2015, to acquire Smith in the hopes that a change of scenery would bring out the best in him.

James Jones was the next player to re-sign with the Cavaliers on July 25, 2015, as he looked to make one final run at a ring. With Jones, Smith, Delladova, Shumpert, Love, James, Irving, and Varejao all back in the fold, the Cavaliers needed to keep adding talent around them as they continued to wait for Tristan Thompson to make up his mind.

On July 10, 2015, they signed point guard Mo Williams to a two-year, $4.3 million contract. Williams had been a huge part of both of LeBron James's MVP seasons during his first stint in town. Williams provided a solid number two scoring punch during those days with the Cavaliers, but this time around he would be counted on to back up Kyrie Irving, who was recovering from his knee injury. Several national pundits believed that had the Cavaliers had Williams instead of Dellavedova in the 2015 playoffs, they would have been able to get past the Warriors after Irving went down.

Mo Williams was born and grew up in Jackson, Mississippi, where he played basketball at Murrah High School. His time there was well spent, as he was recruited to play for coach Mark Gottfried with the Alabama Crimson Tide. Williams proved to be reliable, starting every game his freshman year and averaging 10.4 points and 4.5 assists per game. His great play allowed the Tide to post a record of 27–8, including a 17–0 on their home court, and they captured the SEC regular-season championship. This is also when Williams first encountered postseason disappointment, as the Crimson Tide earned the No. 2 seed in the 2002 NCAA tournament but failed to even get out of the second round, where they were upset by Kent State.

Williams bounced back from that early exit with another strong season in his sophomore campaign. Williams led the team in scoring and assists, averaging 16.4 points and 3.9 assists per game for the 2003 season. Postseason disappointment would once again strike Alabama, their season ending with a first-round loss in the NCAA tournament to Indiana.

He gave up his last two seasons of college eligibility and chose to enter the 2003 NBA draft. That was the draft class that saw LeBron James, Dwyane Wade, Carmelo Anthony, and several other big names get selected. Williams was chosen by the Utah

Jazz in the second round, 47th overall. It was a learning season for Williams, as he averaged five points and 1.3 assists in 14 minutes a game off the bench for the Jazz.

His time with the team was short: the following year he was released by the Jazz and signed with the Milwaukee Bucks. He made an immediate impact in his first season in Milwaukee, averaging 10.2 points and 6.1 assists filling in for injured starting point guard T. J. Ford. His strong play also continued the following season, when he proved to be an impact player off the bench and was called on late in games to make several important shots.

The Bucks noticed Mo Williams making the most of his chances off the bench and chose to trade Ford to the Toronto Raptors, which allowed Williams to become the full-time starter. Williams rewarded the team's faith in him by averaging over 17 points and six assists per game.

The Cavs were one of several teams to have their eye on Williams as he approached free agency in the summer of 2007, but he chose to stay with the Bucks by signing a six-year, $52 million deal. It came as a shock when the Bucks traded him only a little over a year after signing the long-term contract. On August 13, 2008, Williams was traded to the Cavaliers in a three-team, six-player deal also involving the Milwaukee Bucks and the Oklahoma City Thunder that sent Cleveland's Joe Smith and Milwaukee's Desmond Mason to Oklahoma City and Cleveland's Damon Jones and Oklahoma City's Luke Ridnour and Adrian Griffin to Milwaukee.

Just as he had done in Milwaukee, Williams made an immediate impact and finally provided the consistent second scoring threat that the Cavaliers sorely needed to go along with LeBron James. He played in 81 games in his first season with the Cavaliers, averaging 17.8 points and 4.1 assists. His play helped the Cavaliers win the most games in the NBA that season (66) and reach the Eastern Conference finals. He was also chosen to play in the 2009 NBA All-Star Game.

Williams caused some controversy during the Eastern Conference finals when he ran his mouth, guaranteeing a win over the underdog Magic. Orlando would end up winning the series in six games, making Williams eat his words and nullifying the incredible effort put forth by LeBron James, who had a series for the ages in a losing effort, averaging over 38 points per game.

Williams's scoring average dipped a bit during the 2009–10 season, but he was still good for 15.8 points and 5.3 assists a night. The Cavaliers once again recorded the league's best record (61–21) but couldn't get past the Boston Celtics in the second round. The poor playoff outing was yet another postseason disappointment for Williams that seemed to plague his career.

To his credit, Williams showed his loyalty toward Cleveland the following summer after LeBron James embarrassed the city in a nationwide spectacle called "The Decision," when James chose to bolt for Miami. Williams was very vocal sticking up for Cleveland: he didn't hesitate to criticize the events surrounding LeBron's flight from Cleveland and even shot back at insults made by Heat guard Dwyane Wade.

Mo Williams did his best to make the best of a tough situation after James left for Miami and took to the role of leader on the suddenly depleted Cavaliers roster. But as the team's fire sale started midway through the 2010–11 season, Williams was one of the first to go. On February 24, 2011, Williams was traded to the Los Angeles Clippers along with Jamario Moon in exchange for Baron Davis and a first round pick. While Baron Davis was admirable in his half-season with the Cavaliers, it was the pick they acquired that turned out to be a franchise destiny changer. That pick ended up being the first selection in the 2011 NBA draft, which was used on Kyrie Irving.

Williams would not be the man in Los Angeles very long, as they had plans to place him back on the bench when they traded for Chris Paul and claimed Chauncey Billups off waivers, making Williams the Clippers' new sixth man. Williams only stayed with the Clippers one more season before signing with the Portland Trail Blazers. While Portland did reach the NBA playoffs in 2013, it was another disappointment for Williams, because he injured his groin in Game Two of their second round matchup against the San Antonio Spurs and wasn't a factor while the Spurs knocked the Blazers out of the playoffs.

His time with the Trail Blazers was short, and he departed for the Minnesota Timberwolves in the offseason. He never really got the chance to fit in with the Timberwolves; on February 10, 2015, he was traded, along with Troy Daniels and cash considerations, to the Charlotte Hornets in exchange for Gary Neal and Miami's 2019 second-round draft pick. Williams did have one major highlight during his short time in Minnesota when on January 13, 2015, he scored a career-high 52 points on 19 of 33 shooting, breaking the franchise single-game scoring record set by Kevin Love and Corey Brewer by one point in a 110–102 victory over the Indiana Pacers.

The massive scoring effort was good enough to earn him Western Conference Player of the Week honors for the week of January 12–18. Making things even more interesting for the somewhat lost season of Williams was the fact that after the trade to Charlotte, he was named Eastern Conference Player of the Week for games played Monday, March 2, through Sunday, March 8, as he led the Hornets to a 4–0 record that week. This made him the first player to earn the honor in both conferences in the same season since the award was split into two conferences.

Despite playing on a team going nowhere, Williams was desperate to get the attention of better teams, because he knew he would once again be a free agent in the offseason. The July 2015 signing of Williams made the Cavaliers three deep at point guard and also gave him the chance to finish what he started with LeBron during his first stint in Cleveland.

With Williams in the fold, the Big Three returning, and a solid bench, the Cavaliers looked like they were going to be better than they were the previous season. They still awaited an answer from Tristan Thompson but knew that even without Thompson they still had Anderson Varejao coming back from injury along with Mozgov and Love to hold down the frontcourt. The ball was in Thompson's court, and he continued to sit on it. But the Cavaliers still weren't finished and made a play for another esteemed NBA veteran.

Richard Jefferson was the son of Christian missionaries, which kept the youngster on the move often with his parents preaching in various cities around the United States. Once they settled down, Jefferson chose to attend Moon Valley High School in West Phoenix. He fit right in with his classmates and teammates and was a key part of the varsity basketball team that won the 4A State Championship in 1998.

Jefferson was highly recruited coming out of high school and could have had a full ride with any school in the nation because of his immense talent and potential. After careful consideration, he chose to play his college basketball at the University of Arizona. The Wildcats were coached by the legendary Lute Olson, who was one of the greatest basketball coaches in the history of NCAA play. Jefferson's time in Arizona was well spent, as he played three solid seasons under Olson and capped off his junior year by winning the 2001 National Championship. So impressive was his time at Arizona that he was eventually inducted into the Pac-12

Basketball Hall of Honor during the 2012 Pacific-12 Conference Men's Basketball Tournament, in March of 2012.

Jefferson left college as a national champion and was eager to once again take his game to the next level, deciding to enter the 2001 NBA Draft. He was selected 13th overall by the Houston Rockets but was quickly traded to the New Jersey Nets. With the exception of Pau Gasol, selected third overall, and Joe Johnson, tenth, Jefferson would go on to have a better career then the other players selected before him.

The trade to New Jersey was the best thing that could have happened to Richard Jefferson because he was instantly surrounded by top talent on a winning team. The Nets finished with 52 wins, the most of any Eastern Conference team, earning them the number one seed. Thanks in part to his teammates Jason Kidd, Keith Van Horn, and Kenyon Martin, Jefferson was able to be brought along slowly and perform in key spots when called upon. The Nets beat the Indiana Pacers in a heated five-game series that went the distance. They crushed the Charlotte Hornets in the next round, winning in five games. They beat the Boston Celtics in a classic six-game series to earn a trip to the NBA Finals against the two-time defending champion Los Angeles Lakers. Their magic ran out in the finals, and they were swept, but not before Jefferson could have a solid rookie season.

Jefferson finished his rookie season averaging 9.4 points in 24-plus minutes a game. His numbers would increase dramatically the following season with 15.5 points and 6.4 rebounds a game. His performance was a key reason the Nets returned to the NBA Finals, where they were swept by the San Antonio Spurs.

Jefferson would continue to improve each season. He averaged 18.5 points a game in his third season and then topped that with a career high in 2004–2005 when he averaged 22.2 points and 7.3 rebounds despite battling injuries several times that season.

The Nets failed to return to the NBA Finals during that stretch and eventually let go of their head coach Byron Scott in favor of Lawrence Frank. Jefferson's game continued to improve under the new coach, as he became one of the best all-around players in the league.

Jefferson combined his skills with Jason Kidd and Vince Carter to form one of the most imposing lineups in the NBA in 2006–07. The Nets had the talent to return to and win the NBA championship but ran into LeBron James and the Cleveland Cavaliers in the second round and were knocked out in six games. After losing to the Cavaliers, they never really returned to form the following season, and Jefferson was traded to the Milwaukee Bucks in the offseason for Yi Jianlian and Bobby Simmons. Thus began a rebuilding stage for the Nets, and the next chapter of Jefferson's career.

Richard Jefferson had intended to play his entire career as a Net. He was a very loyal teammate and, from all accounts, an outstanding member of the community. It was a culture shock for him to leave New Jersey for Milwaukee, but it was rumored that he was excited to play with fellow All-Star Michael Redd. Jefferson's stay there would only last a season, after which he was traded to the San Antonio Spurs for Bruce Bowen, Kurt Thomas, and Fabricio Oberto on June 23, 2009.

He spent two and a half seasons in the Lone Star State until he was traded yet again. On March 15, 2012, the Golden State Warriors traded newly-acquired Stephen Jackson for Jefferson, along with T. J. Ford and a conditional first-round pick. Jefferson only spent one season as a Warrior before he was sent to the Utah Jazz, along with teammates Brandon Rush and Andris Biedrins, in a three-team trade involving the Denver Nuggets.

He would spend one season in Utah and then one in Dallas before Cleveland signed him on August 5, 2015. It was clear that Cleveland would be his last stop, where he would get one more chance at a ring and provide veteran leadership off the bench.

The Cavaliers wouldn't need much out of him, but his savvy leadership and ability to knock down the clutch shot were too tempting for them to pass up, so they signed him.

With the sole exception of Tristan Thompson, the roster was set going into training camp. LeBron James, still champing at the bit to get the bad taste of another NBA Finals loss out of his mouth, called for a team minicamp at his gym down in Miami in the month of September, as a way to unite the team and work together in preparation for the upcoming season. Much was being said of Thompson's holdout, but James was doing his best to stay out of it and keep his team focused on the task at hand. Thompson was invited to the camp, but the big man chose to decline until his contract status was clearer.

After the camp ended, it was now time to begin the official training camp held by the team. The guards on the roster were Kyrie Irving, Mo Williams, Joe Harris, J. R. Smith, Matthew Dellavedova, James Jones, and Iman Shumpert, along with forwards LeBron James, Richard Jefferson, Kevin Love, and Anderson Varejao. Holding down the middle would be centers Timofey Mozgov and Sasha Kaun, with still no sign of Tristan Thompson.

One thing Thompson had going for him was durability; he was almost never hurt and played significant minutes in every single game for the Cavaliers, including the playoffs the prior season. Health was a prime concern heading into the season, as the championship run was cut short because of injuries the previous June. The injury bug would strike again just days before training camp, when starting shooting guard Iman Shumpert badly injured his right wrist during a routine workout in the gym. He required surgery to repair a ruptured muscle and was scheduled to miss twelve to fourteen weeks.

It was a bitter pill for the Cavaliers to swallow, since they already knew that Irving would miss the start of the year due to his knee injury from the Finals series against the Golden State Warriors. Both starters in the backcourt, Shumpert and Irving, would start the season on the inactive list. This would make Mo Williams's role at the point guard position and J. R. Smith's at shooting guard that much more important to the team's overall success.

Aware that they would be thin to start the season at both point guard and shooting guard, David Griffin searched for one more player to add to the bench for depth at both positions. The man he found was Jared Cunningham, a player whom his predecessor, Chris Grant, had selected in the 2012 draft out of Oregon State.

Cunningham came to Oregon State listed as the No. 14 point guard and the No. 76 player in the nation in 2009. He had a stellar high school career at San Leandro High School, where he stepped onto the national stage his junior year, averaging 17.8 points, 4.5 rebounds, and 3.3 assists per game. He continued to turn the heads of college scouts as a senior by averaging 20.4 points, 6.3 rebounds, and 2.6 assists per game and earned academic All-America honors.

He had a slow freshman year at Oregon State, seeing limited playing time, but was still able to average 6.2 points, 2.0 rebounds, and 0.9 assists per game. Things improved in his sophomore year, when Cunningham averaged 14.2 points, 3.1 rebounds, 2.1 assists, and 2.9 steals per game. His defense didn't go unnoticed, either, as he was named to the All-Pac-10 Second Team and the Pac-10 All-Defensive-Team. He was also named to the 2011 Pac-10 All-Tournament Team after averaging 23.5 points per game.

Cunningham decided to stick around for his junior year and he was wise to do so, averaging 17.9 points, 3.8 rebounds, 2.8 assists, and 2.5 steals per game. He led the Pac-12 in steals for the second consecutive season and also finished ninth nationally. Cunningham was also named to the All-Pac-12 First Team,

LeBron James was a two time NBA regular-season MVP during his first stint in Cleveland. *Photo by Kenny Roda.*

James did the unthinkable and left for Miami in the summer of 2010. *Photo by Kenny Roda.*

Kyrie Irving sizes up another victory celebration after a huge playoff win over Toronto. *Photo by Kenny Roda.*

Kevin Love waits to congratulate his teammates after a playoff win against Atlanta. *Photo by Kenny Roda.*

LeBron James's massive wingspan makes him a great defender.
Photo courtesy of neosportsinsiders.com

Cleveland's Big Three: LeBron James, Kyrie Irving, and Kevin Love.
Photo by Kenny Roda.

Quicken Loans Arena, "The Q," home of champions. *Photo by Kenny Roda.*

The Cavs swept the Atlanta Hawks in both the 2015 and 2016 playoffs.
Photo by Matt Medley.

Veteran forward Richard Jefferson was a great addition in 2015–16. *Photo courtesy of neosportsinsiders.com.*

J. R. Smith spots up for another three-point shot. *Photo courtesy of neosportsinsiders.com.*

The trade for Iman Shumpert and J. R. Smith in January 2015 really paid off. *Photo by the author.*

Mo Williams returned to the Cavs in 2015–16 after being traded away five seasons earlier. *Photo by the author.*

General manager David Griffin had the responsibility of putting together a team around LeBron that could contend for the championship. *Photo courtesy of neosportsinsiders.com.*

Head coach David Blatt was let go midway through the 2015–16 season with a record of 30–11. *Photo courtesy of neosportsinsiders.com.*

Tyronn Lue took over from Blatt and led the Cavs to the title. *Photo courtesy of neosportsinsiders.com.*

The entire city of Cleveland was All In! *Photo by Kenny Roda.*

Channing Frye was a key trade-deadline addition in 2016. *AP Photo/Tony Dejak.*

Tristan Thompson slams one home! *AP Photo/Tony Dejak.*

Timofey Mozgov towered over opponents. *AP Photo/Tony Dejak.*

Matthew Dellavedova was a fan favorite. *AP Photo/Tony Dejak.*

Iman Shumpert drives to the lane against the Toronto Raptors in the Eastern Conference finals. *AP Photo/Tony Dejak.*

LeBron James takes a free throw in Game Three of the 2016 NBA Finals. *Photo by Kenny Roda.*

The crucial Game Six of the 2016 NBA Finals tips off. *Photo by Kenny Roda.*

Golden State's Stephen Curry leaves the court
after getting ejected from Game Six.
Photo by Kenny Roda.

Kyrie Irving walks off after a huge Game Six victory against the Golden State Warriors. *Photo by Kenny Roda.*

Time to celebrate after winning Game Six.
Photo by Kenny Roda.

James and Love embrace as the clock hits zero in Game Seven of the 2016 NBA Finals. *AP Photo/ Eric Risberg*

The 2016 NBA Champion Cleveland Cavaliers. *AP Photo/Eric Risberg*

1.3 million people turned out for the championship parade on June 22.
AP Photo/Gene J. Puskar.

the Pac-12 All-Defensive Team, and the Pac-12 All-Tournament team for the second consecutive season.

He was selected by the Cavs with the 24th overall pick in the 2012 NBA draft. He would not stay a Cavalier for long: his draft rights were then traded with Jae Crowder and Bernard James to the Dallas Mavericks in exchange for Tyler Zeller and Kelenna Azubuike on draft night. He only played eight games for the Mavericks before being traded to the Atlanta Hawks in a draft-night deal in 2013. The Hawks cut him after a couple of brief assignments with the Bakersfield Jam of the NBA Development League.

Cunningham's professional journey continued after he was cut by the Hawks. On March 31, 2014, Cunningham signed a 10-day contract with the Sacramento Kings, and he signed with the Kings for the rest of the season on April 10. He played well enough that in July 2014, he joined the Kings for the 2014 NBA Summer League, but his luck ran out and he did not receive a new contract offer from the team. He was determined to stay in the NBA and on September 29 signed with the Los Angeles Clippers. His stint with the Clippers was cut short when he was traded, along with the draft rights to Cenk Akyol and cash considerations, to the Philadelphia 76ers in exchange for the draft rights to Sergei Lishouk on Januarry 7, 2015. The 76ers had no interest in keeping him, and he was waived later that day. After playing for the Utah Jazz in the 2015 NBA Summer League, he returned to the team that originally drafted him when he signed with the Cleveland Cavaliers on September 28, 2015.

He had only 40 games of NBA experience between Dallas, Atlanta, Los Angeles, and Sacramento, but it didn't matter to the Cavaliers, because they needed an extra body to come off the bench. Less than a week into the regular season, Cunningham, due to circumstances beyond his control, would be in the starting lineup.

CHAPTER 3

Hot Start

THE CAVALIERS' 2015 PRESEASON WAS very lackluster. LeBron James, resting his ailing back, and Kevin Love, who looked fine and appeared to be fully recovered, only appeared in two games apiece. With the preseason wrapping up, Tristan Thompson finally ended his four-month holdout and agreed to a five-year, $82 million contract on October 22. It was a substantial amount of money for a backup forward. It was almost as if he were treated as a really expensive insurance policy fund in the event Love got hurt again. Thompson missed all of training camp and the pre-season that saw the Cavaliers win only one of seven games.

The drama was over, Thompson was re-signed, Love was healthy, and the Cavaliers were ready to complete a champion-ship quest that began in July of 2014. Cleveland was playing in an improved Eastern Conference, yet still favored by many to win it. The Atlanta Hawks looked to build on their confer-ence-best record from the previous season with returning starters

Kyle Korver, Jeff Teague, Paul Millsap, and Al Horford. The Washington Wizards also looked better than ever with a healthy John Wall and Bradley Beal, one of the NBA's best backcourts. The Miami Heat attempted to bounce back from a rough 2014–15 with the returning Chris Bosh and Dwyane Wade combined with Goran Dragic.

The Indiana Pacers also gave the Eastern Conference another piece of credibility with Paul George returning after missing almost the entire season. The Detroit Pistons appeared to be vastly improved heading into the new season with Marcus Morris, Ersan Ilyasova, and Andre Drummond. The Milwaukee Bucks looked a lot better than people realized. Coach Jason Kidd had the likes of second-year phenom Jabari Parker to go along with former rookie of the year Michael Carter-Williams and Greg Monroe.

The Toronto Raptors held one of the best records in the league in 2014-2015 until a late-season collapse and were aiming to get things back in order for the upcoming season. The Raptors proved how good they were by winning their first five games led by Kyle Lowry, DeMar DeRozan, DeMarre Carroll, and Jonas Valanciunas. Many in the national media felt that the Raptors had a good of chance of bringing an NBA title to the great white north. With the improving Bucks, Pacers, and Pistons to go along with the Wizards, Hawks, Raptors, and Heat, the Eastern Conference was no longer seen as a cupcake.

Perhaps their biggest challenge would come from their opening night opponent, the Chicago Bulls. The Cavaliers were asked to open the season on the road in Chicago. The game was widely hyped, with President Barack Obama in attendance.

The Bulls were still fuming from being knocked out by LeBron James the prior spring for the fourth time in six seasons, dating back to his original stint in Cleveland. They were the only team, before the finals, to lead Cleveland in a series, and if it weren't for a LeBron James buzzer beater, they possibly could have held a 3–1 lead. Losing that series led to the firing of their head coach, Tom Thibodeau.

To replace him, they brought in former Iowa State University head coach Fred Hoiberg, who served as the Minnesota Timberwolves' vice president for basketball operations before beginning his coaching career. Hoiberg had a 10-year NBA playing career with stints in Chicago, Indiana, and Minnesota. The Bulls were hoping he would be the man to help them finally get past LeBron James and into the NBA Finals.

The Bulls' roster was solid, but also aging in many areas. The starting backcourt consisted of former MVP Derrick Rose, who was still one of the best in the game but had a very hard time staying healthy, missing parts of the last four seasons nursing injuries that limited him to a total of only 100 regular-season games. He missed the entire 2012–13 season due to a knee injury. He would begin the new season wearing a face mask after suffering a fractured left orbital bone during the preseason. If Rose could ever stay healthy, the Bulls would be a serious threat.

Rose's backcourt partner was Jimmy Butler, who had a strong defensive showing against LeBron James in the 2015 playoffs and looked to continue it in 2016. Chicago's formidable lineup also boasted perennial All-Stars Joakim Noah and Pau Gasol.

Just as it did in 2014–15, the season opener did not go well for the Cavaliers. The Bulls got off to a red-hot start and led, 26–17, after the first quarter. James got off to a slow start and came out of the game after missing seven of his first eight shots. He would eventually re-enter the game and get his wind back to the tune of 25 points, 10 rebounds, and five assists. It wasn't enough, as the Cavaliers could never come all the way back and ended up losing the game in the final moments, 97–95. They had a chance for one last shot, but Jimmy Butler broke up an inbounds pass intended for James, and the Bulls were able to hold on. Kevin Love looked good in his first game back with 18 points, eight rebounds, and two blocked shots.

It was a tough loss, but the biggest issue was the fact that Blatt again wasn't able to draw up an effective inbounds play at the end of a game, a major flaw the previous season. Despite his inability to get the inbounds pass to James, Mo Williams had a very good game in his first night back in a Cavaliers uniform during the regular season by scoring 19 points to go along with seven assists.

The Cavaliers would bounce back from the tough loss with a huge road win the very next night in Memphis again the Grizzlies. The Cavaliers took no prisoners as they raced to a 26–10 lead after the first quarter. The final result was a 106–76 blowout victory. Love dominated from start to finish with 17 points and 13 rebounds.

Kevin Love's surgically repaired shoulder seemed to be holding up quite well in the early going. He was quoted as saying, "If it was going to go against two teams, it was going to be those two teams. I guess for a couple tests coming right out of the gate, those are them. Definitely got hit, got pulled, got my arm locked a few times and I'm pretty sore too, so it's definitely been tested and I'm sure it will continue to be."

A sold-out crowd packed Quicken Loans Arena on October 30, 2015, to cheer on the Cavaliers in their home opener against the hated Miami Heat. Even with LeBron back in town, Miami was still public enemy number one because of the four years James spent with them.

The Cavaliers rolled from start to finish, keeping the crowd on their feet the entire night. James scored 29 points while Kevin Love added 24 with 14 rebounds, as they won their home opener, 102–92. James was 13 of 19 from the field for Cleveland, which pulled away midway through the second half.

Love's performance was so sharp that James was quoted after the game as saying that Love, and not himself, would be the main scoring focus this season. No one took him seriously, but it was nice of him to at least attempt to put someone else in front of himself in the press.

"Kevin Love is our main focal point," said James. "We want to get Kev to know how great he is and how good he is for our team. He showed again tonight why he's one of the best power forwards in our league."

It wasn't the only strange thing to come out of LeBron's mouth that day, as earlier in the evening during pregame shootaround, he was heard claiming that he was planning on playing in all 82 regular season games. This was a far cry from his talk in preseason that he needed rest and hoped for reduced minutes. It was getting to the point that LeBron was saying things for effect based on what day it was. As for the Cavs, it didn't matter much because they just kept winning, eventually running their record to 8–1 with eight consecutive wins after dropping the opener in Chicago. They would continue to roll from there with very few issues, losing a few here and there, but still winning most of the time.

As the team prepared to take on the visiting Atlanta Hawks on November 21 in a rematch of the previous season's Eastern Conference finals, they received some bad news when starting shooting guard J. R. Smith was accused of choking a high school student in New York at 4 a.m. after a game there earlier in the month. The *New York Daily News* reported that 19-year-old Justin Brown had made the accusation, telling police that after Smith ignored a request for a picture, Brown heckled him and the player responded by shoving him against a wall and putting his hands around his throat. It was the latest in a long line of questionable actions by Smith that gave him a reputation as an immature and self-absorbed troublemaker. It was another clear sign that the talent Smith showed on the court was simply not worth his horrendous behavior off of it.

Even during a big win over Atlanta, the Cavaliers still could not escape drama, when late in the game with a huge lead, LeBron walked off the court in frustration over a turnover. They were up big and he was playing well, no one subbed in for him since he didn't tell anyone he was walking off the court, and the selfish move out of frustration led to a technical foul and free points for the Hawks. Had the game been close, a stunt like that could have really cost them. It showed total disrespect to his coach and teammates in front of a large home crowd.

Earlier in the week, LeBron had proclaimed that Blatt was as good as any coach in the NBA, then days later he once again showed him little respect. Despite those incidents, Cleveland continued to roll, improving their record to 13–4 and reaching the cusp of getting Kyrie Irving and Iman Shumpert back shortly. One had to wonder: what would happen if eventually the controversy continued, and the winning didn't?

The Cavaliers knew things were about to get tougher, since their next four contests were against playoff-quality competition. They would host the Washington Wizards before leaving for a two-game road trip against the New Orleans Pelicans and Miami Heat before returning home to face the Portland Trail Blazers. They had to be careful not to overlook so many good teams, especially with the prospect of a Christmas Day game against the Golden State Warriors, currently 18–0, looming. That contest was only twenty-seven days away, and the national media was already hyping it. Only one question remained, not if the Warriors would remain unbeaten by the time of the game, but rather, would Kyrie Irving be back for it?

CHAPTER 4

Kyrie Returns

As the NBA Finals rematch with the Warriors approached, Shumpert and Irving continued to practice with the team at full speed but still hadn't been cleared for in-game competition. It would only be a matter of time before they returned, but the Cavaliers were playing their cards close to the vest as to when.

Shumpert returned first, coming off the bench when the Cavaliers traveled to Orlando to take on the Magic on Friday, December 11. The return of Shumpert was just the emotional lift the team needed, as they crushed the Magic, 111–76, in a game that was never close. The Cavaliers put the game away with a massive third quarter, outscoring the Magic, 30–15. Shumpert played just under 25 minutes and scored 14 points.

The Cavaliers stayed hot, rattling off four more wins in a row to extend their winning streak to six games before the highly anticipated Christmas Day matchup against the Golden State Warriors. It was during that stretch that Kyrie Irving made his long awaited return on Sunday, December 20, against the lowly, one-win Philadelphia 76ers. The Cavaliers blew out the visiting 76ers, 108–86. If it was good to see Shumpert back in the lineup, it was great to see their All-Star point guard Irving return. He was limited to 17 minutes of playing time, but he did start and score 12 points in his season debut. His kneecap appeared to be fine, and Cleveland would need it to be if they hoped to make another run at the championship.

A few days after Irving's return to the lineup, the Cavaliers won their last tune-up game before the Golden State showdown with a mechanical 91–84 win over the visiting New York Knicks. They were heading into the Christmas Day showdown with a record of 19–7, good enough for the best record in the Eastern Conference. It would typically be up there for the best record in the entire NBA if it weren't for the fact that their opponent had only one loss against 27 victories. The Warriors were about as close to unbeatable as a team could be early on. They started the season with 24 straight wins and were running teams out of the gym with a fast-paced, high-scoring offense that no one could contend with.

The talk around the league was that the only team that could possibly unseat the defending NBA champions from their throne was a fully healthy Cleveland Cavaliers squad. Cleveland took the Warriors to six games in the 2015 NBA Finals and firmly believed that they would have won the entire series if they were at full strength. This was about as big of a showdown as a mid-season Christmas Day game could be. It harkened back to the Chicago Bulls, led by Michael Jordan, going against the New York Knicks, led by Patrick Ewing, on Christmas Day games in the 1990s, back when there was only one game on Christmas, and not five, as under the current structure. The game was big; and after

Christmas dinner was digested, the presents were passed out, and the fat man in the red suit was on his way back to the North Pole, it was time for business!

Just as they did to every other opponent all season, the Warriors came out running, shooting, and scoring at a wicked pace. They outscored the Cavaliers, 28–19, in the first quarter alone. The Warriors were already on pace for 112 points, which was right around their average. The Cavaliers were stunned but knew that their defense was strong enough to put a stop to the Warriors' scoring spree, and they went out and did just that, holding Golden State to 17 points in the second quarter and 19 in the third quarter.

The only problem was, with the extended effort on defense, their offense suffered and they only shot 2 of 17 from behind the arc in the first half. It didn't improve much in the third quarter, and they still trailed, 64–59, heading into the fourth quarter. Holding the Warriors to only 64 points was extremely impressive, considering that they had sometimes reached that total by halftime. The Cavs still needed an offensive boost and looked to get it from whoever was willing to help.

That man wouldn't be Kevin Love, because he had been held to only 10 points, despite giving a maximum effort on the boards with 18 rebounds. Kyrie Irving still looked rusty, as well, only scoring 13 points. They managed to close to within four points with a little more than two minutes to go, but LeBron James missed two foul shots and they never recovered, eventually falling to the Warriors, 89–83. James played well, scoring 25 points with nine rebounds, but those two missed foul shots proved to be costly.

One bright spot in this defeat was the superior defensive effort shown by the Cavaliers over the final three quarters. They held the powerful Warriors to only 89 points, well below their season average. They also held their two best scorers, Stephen Curry and Klay Thompson, to fewer than 20 points each. They proved once again that if you play the Warriors physically, they could be stopped.

If the Cavaliers had shot even halfway decently, the game might have been a rout in their favor. Poor shooting buried them, as they only shot 30 of 95 from the field (32 percent) and 5 of 30 (17 percent) from behind the arc, by far and away their worst shooting game of the season. It would have to improve if they had any chance to take down Golden State should a rematch occur in the Finals.

It is never easy for a team in any sport to travel across the country to play a game, let alone on Christmas Day against the defending world champions. The Cavaliers showed the effects of the painful loss the next night, failing to resemble a competitive team as they were handed a brutal 105–76 loss at the hands of the Trail Blazers in Portland. It was the second half of a back-to-back, and Cleveland's legs, hearts, and minds simply weren't there, allowing the Trail Blazers to capitalize.

The Cavs finished the 2015 part of their schedule with a 21–9 record, good for first place in the Central Division. It was a sharp contrast from the previous year, when they went into the New Year's holiday in the middle of a collapse and serious doubt as LeBron left for a sabbatical in Miami and the fans and press called for Blatt's dismissal. They didn't have any of those problems this season, and things looked very bright for the final fifty-two regular season games ahead of them.

A few weeks later, they had won the first four games of a six-game road trip when they arrived in San Antonio for another big test on the schedule. The Spurs were 34–6 on the season and only two-and-a-half games behind Golden State for the league's best record. San Antonio had their Big Three of Tony

Parker, Tim Duncan, and Manu Ginobili back in full force for another run at the title. With the addition of LaMarcus Aldridge in the offseason, they were as dangerous as ever.

The Cavs jumped out to a 15-point lead in the first quarter behind some hot shooting, but the Spurs eventually climbed back in the game. In a game of runs, San Antonio caught fire in the fourth quarter, winning, 99–95. The Spurs were led by Tony Parker, who had 24 points while playing great defense against Kyrie Irving, who was held to 16 points and looked lost trying to cover Parker at times. Love was only 4 of 10 on the night for 10 points. They would go on to win the final game of the trip the next night in Houston, 91–77.

Awaiting the Cavaliers upon returning home was a rematch with the Warriors. A combination of bad defense and maybe even some tired legs led to the Cavaliers being blown out and embarrassed at home in a nationally televised game. Golden State destroyed Cleveland from the opening tip, going on a 12–2 run to start the game, and they never looked back.

The Cavaliers trailed, 70–44, at the half, as Stephen Curry burned them for 21 points. Tristan Thompson, the 82 million-dollar man, failed to score and picked up four personal fouls. Love and Irving combined for only five points. Things would get worse in the second half, and they would ultimately lose, 132–98, in an embarrassing and uninspired effort. "Stuff" was about to hit the fan. LeBron was spotted on the bench venting his frustration to assistant coach Tyronn Lue. It was a crushing loss, and in a matter of days the long-term effects would be felt.

Three nights later, the Cavaliers showed their grit and bounced back with a big win at home on national television against the Los Angeles Clippers, 115-102. In many ways, it was their most impressive win of the season, as five players scored in double digits. James and Smith led the way with 22 points each, Irving added 21, Kevin Love had 18 points (with 16 rebounds), and Mozgov scored 11 points in limited playing time. It was a total team effort, the exact way Blatt wanted them to play, but it wasn't enough; and the unthinkable would happen the very next day.

CHAPTER 5

When First Place Isn't Enough

ON JANUARY 22, 2016, THE Cavaliers were 30–11 and had the best record in the Eastern Conference. They had dominated most of the conference opponents they faced and were a staggering 16–2 at home. The only cause for concern was the blowout loss to the Golden State Warriors earlier in the week. It resulted in a players-only meeting, and within days, head coach David Blatt was fired.

To say fans and media were shocked would be an understatement, but sadly for Blatt, the writing was on the wall. LeBron James never missed a chance to throw him under the bus and never once publicly gave him his full support. James would give him the occasional praise, only to knock him for something days later. Blatt could be criticized for benching Kevin Love in the fourth quarter of games and giving too much playing time to Matthew Dellavedova and not nearly enough to Timofey Mozgov, but all things considered, those minor flaws shouldn't have caused the Cavaliers to fire a coach who led them to a 30–11 record and had guided an injury-plagued team to a 2–1 series lead during the prior year's NBA Finals. It was a bold move for GM David Griffith and owner Dan Gilbert (with LeBron James's blessing) to make.

It was comical that James told several national media outlets that he was never consulted and had nothing to do with it. It was nearly impossible for the team not to have consulted with him. It wasn't long after the firing of Blatt that rumors about Love being traded began, as well. Why would a team playing such great basketball resort to such major changes if it wasn't the result of panic? Whatever the case may be, it was a risky move to hand the team over to assistant coach Tyronn Lue, but as their motto said, the Cavaliers were about to go "all in" with Lue.

Blatt issued a statement released by Priority Sports and Entertainment later that day that read, "I am very grateful to have had the opportunity to serve as the Head Coach of the Cleveland Cavaliers. I'd like to thank Dan Gilbert and David Griffin for giving me this opportunity and am honored to have worked with an amazing group of players from LeBron James, Kyrie Irving, and Kevin Love through our entire roster. I'd also like to express my extreme gratitude to my coaching staff. I am indebted to them for their professionalism, hard work, loyalty, and friendship. I am proud of what we have accomplished since I have been the Head Coach and wish the Cavaliers nothing but the best this season and beyond."

Griffin gave several reasons for the move at his post-firing press conference, the second of which he has held since taking the job. He didn't like the dynamic, and he didn't think any more time would change it. He was confident that enough time remained in the season for the Cavs to fix internal problems and become a legitimate championship contender. The *Cleveland Plain Dealer*'s Dennis Manoloff made an excellent point in his article following the firing, when he wrote, "In a presser Friday, Griffin essentially made two strong points without actually saying the words: Cavs players like/respect Lue and didn't like/respect Blatt. Cavs players have no more excuses. The fall guy, Blatt, is gone. It is time for the players to earn their hefty paychecks and play like a championship team."

Yahoo Sports columnist Adrian Wojnarowski, who first reported the firing, wrote that he saw it coming a mile away in his follow-up column later in the day: "Before David Blatt ever conducted his first training camp practice in September 2014, Cleveland Cavaliers star LeBron James and his agent, Rich Paul, had the coach's succession plan in place: Mark Jackson. From the beginning, the Klutch Sports campaign to puncture Blatt's standing as head coach had been as relentless as it was ruthless. James is one of the great leaders in pro sports, and he directed the Cavaliers how he wanted them: in complete defiance of Blatt. Once James' camp realized that Jackson would never be considered as coach—nor would Lue leave his representation to join Klutch Sports agency, despite overtures—Lue became a compromise choice for James' group, sources said. They started pushing for Lue to replace Blatt last season, and grew louder in those calls in recent days and weeks." Wojnarowski also stated that James had become more vocal in his opposition to Blatt during both recent practices and games.

Highly controversial Cavaliers beat reporter Chris Haynes of the *Plain Dealer* attempted to give his "insider's" view on the firing: "Blatt didn't have the necessary relationship with his guys to get players to buy in. Lue is expected to hold players accountable. He's not afraid to give James a piece of his mind. Players from 1 down to 15 will be held responsible . . . Lue's connection with the players is rock solid, with a reputation for understanding how to manage personalities. He has played with two of the league's biggest personalities—Michael Jordan and Kobe Bryant—and he's been coached by some of the greats." Haynes also claimed that Blatt's firing might have come even earlier if they hadn't beaten the Phoenix Suns two nights after their dreadful effort at Portland.

WHBC 1480 Radio host Kenny Roda had these thoughts on the coaching switch: "I wasn't as surprised as everybody else. I thought something could happen after the Golden State loss at home by such a large margin. I just wasn't sure it would happen this quick."

Rick Carlisle, the head of the NBA Coaches Association who led the Dallas Mavericks in a victorious NBA Finals effort against LeBron James and the Heat in the summer of 2011, had these thoughts: "I'm embarrassed for our league that David Blatt was fired, he will be highly sought after, he was a good coach and man."

Fans reaction was mixed, ranging from outrage to enthusiasm about the switch. Some sided with management, while others blamed James.

Former Cavaliers center Brendan Haywood agreed with the firing of Blatt and was not surprised based on what he saw the previous season while on the bench. In a SiriusXM radio interview, Haywood was quoted as saying, "Coach Blatt was very hesitant to challenge LeBron James. It was one of those situations where, being a rookie coach, and LeBron being bigger than life, it was a little too much for him. I remember we had James Jones [talk] to Coach about how, 'Hey, you can't just skip over when LeBron James makes a mistake in the film room.' Because we all see it.

"And we're like, 'Hey, you didn't say anything about that. You're going to correct when Matthew Dellavedova's not in the right spot. You're going to say something when Tristan Thompson's not in the right spot. Well, we see a fast break and LeBron didn't get back on defense or there's a rotation and he's supposed to be there, and you just keep rolling the film and the whole room is quiet.' We see that as players. That's when . . . as a player, you start to lose respect for a coach.

"Slowly but surely, that respect started chipping away where he would kind of be scared to correct LeBron in film sessions. When he would call every foul for LeBron in practice. Those type of things add up. Guys are like, 'C'mon man, are you scared of him?'"

The Tyronn Lue Era wouldn't start with a layup by any means, as his first night on the job he would be leading Cleveland against the visiting Chicago Bulls. The Bulls had always been a thorn in Cleveland's side dating back to the 1980s, and they looked to spoil the debut of the new head coach. It didn't take long for the Cleveland fans watching to realize that even with a new coach, the Bulls would remain a problem, as they upset the Cavs, 96–83, in a game that was a blowout from the middle of the first half on.

The biggest concern that arose from the game was the lack of scoring. The Cavaliers were flat from the beginning, and no adjustments were made to get a spark going. They looked lost on offense, and it appeared it would become an uphill battle to install the new fast-paced offense that Lue was looking to run. He was quick to criticize his team after the game, pointing out that they would need to get in better shape to run his offense.

LeBron James had a stellar game with 26 points, 13 rebounds, and nine assists along with a block and three steals. The rest of the team seemed to struggle in the new offense, as Kyrie Irving was held to 11 points and only two assists. Kevin Love scored 14 points but looked flat at times.

The largest cause of concern was a team total of 4-for-24 from the three point line and 9 of 22 from the charity stripe. Lue didn't hesitate to rip into his team after the game. The lack of hustle, poor shooting, and sloppy play was not exactly the change that David Griffin was looking for with the switch to Lue.

The Cavaliers managed to bounce back from the awful first showing under Lue to win the next five straight against Minnesota, Phoenix, and San Antonio at home, and the Detroit Pistons and Indiana Pacers on the road. They scored over 110 points in each game.

The main reason for switching to Lue was his ability to hold players accountable, regardless of their position on the roster. Another motive was the fast-paced offense he promised to bring with him. Perhaps the biggest benefactor of the switch was Kevin Love. After struggling against the Timberwolves and Bulls, he caught fire and scored 21 against the Suns, 29 against the Pistons, 21 against the Spurs, and 19 against the Pacers. This was the high-scoring Kevin Love that Cavaliers fans hoped to see on a nightly basis going forward, the same player that David Blatt held back so many times now finally being allowed to blossom.

Lue was 5–1 in his first ten days as coach, and the Cavaliers appeared to be headed back in the right direction. One negative trait former coaches David Blatt and Mike Brown both shared was failing to make halftime adjustments when needed; Lue would have to avoid that same mistake if he hoped to lead the Cavaliers to a championship.

Kyrie Irving excelled in the new offense, and his game-high 32 points helped the Cavaliers blow out the visiting Sacramento Kings, 120–100, on February 8. Perhaps Irving was finally starting to get his legs back after sitting out the first twenty-four games, or perhaps he was angered by not being selected to the All-Star game; in any event, he was showing flashes of his old self, and it came at the perfect time for Coach Lue and the rest of the team.

He remained hot two nights later by scoring a season-high 35 points against the visiting Los Angeles Lakers.

While Irving was heating up, future first-ballot Hall of Famer Kobe Bryant was winding down the final season of his legendary career. Bryant had announced that this would be his final season and was making the most of his farewell tour. His numbers were significantly down, but it didn't stop the fans from making every effort possible to see him. He gained the most votes to appear in the upcoming All-Star Game, and the nosebleed upper-deck seats for the game in Cleveland were going for up to $500. Fans were not going to miss their last chance to see LeBron vs. Kobe up close.

While the Cavaliers led from start to finish, up by 19 after three quarters and seemingly cruising to victory thanks to the 35 points from Kyrie Irving and 29 from James, they didn't escape from the game unscathed. Kevin Love had been off to another hot start with eight points, six rebounds, and three assists in less than 19 minutes when he got his arm caught underneath Kobe Bryant's while in the post. "At the time I really didn't know what it was," Love said. "It's like when you get hit in the funny bone in your elbow, it's just shooting pain. It felt like fire was running down my arm. It's just a stinger." It was the same shoulder Love had dislocated in the first round of the previous season's playoffs when Boston center Kelly Olynyk pulled it from the socket in a dirty play that ended his season. Postgame word was that Love wasn't expected to miss too much time when the regular season resumed following that weekend's All-Star break.

Speaking of the All-Star break, it wasn't lost on the Cavaliers players, coaches, and fans that LeBron James was the only Cleveland player going to Toronto to play in the game. The Cavaliers held the Eastern Conference's best record at 38–14. The closest to them in the East was Toronto at 35–17. The snubs made it clear that until the Cavaliers could win an NBA championship, they would never receive the proper attention and respect, and would just be seen as LeBron and the rest of the guys. Coach Lue and the rest of the team would work hard in the second half of the season as they aimed to achieve that goal and erase that image.

CHAPTER 6

Playing Out the String

For the Cleveland Cavaliers, the second half of the NBA season would be about more than just playing out the string and trying to stay healthy. Not only did they need to win to secure the number one seed in the Eastern Conference, they also needed to look good doing it and prove that the coaching switch was the smart move. They couldn't afford to overlook opponents as they did at times in the first half of the season. It was a big knock against them that they weren't taking personal responsibility for losses and holding one another accountable. Coach Lue's mission would be to change all that and get the team running on all cylinders heading into the playoffs.

It seemed as though every time the Cavaliers were looking for a fresh start, the Chicago Bulls were first up on the schedule. They lost to the Bulls in the season opener and also in Tyronn Lue's coaching debut in mid-January. The Bulls always seemed to have the kryptonite to stop them, but this time was different as the Cavaliers led from start to finish in a dominant 106–95 victory.

It was an impressive win considering they were able to stay focused despite the fact that earlier in the day they traded away Anderson Varejao, their longest-tenured player. "Wild Thing" spent 12 seasons with the Cavs, endearing himself to his teammates with his hustle and becoming a fan favorite. The Cavaliers received 6-foot-11 Channing Frye from the Orlando Magic as part of a three-team trade involving the Portland Trail Blazers in which they parted with Varejao, Jared Cunningham, and two future draft picks including a first-rounder. Frye had been a highly-recruited player out of St. Mary's High School in Phoenix, Arizona. The high expectations began for Frye when he was rated as the No. 98 recruit in the nation by Hoop Scoop and the No. 13 center in the country by Fast Break Recruiting Service.

In his senior year at St. Mary's in 2000–01, Frye averaged 22 points, 15 rebounds, six blocks, and three assists per game, and he led the school to the 2001 Class 5A state championship with a 30–3 record. It came as no surprise that he was named Player of the Year by the *Arizona Republic* and the Arizona Gatorade Player of the Year while earning fourth-team *Parade* All-America and McDonald's All-America honors.

He earned Pac-10 All-Freshman Team honors after averaging 9.5 points, 6.3 rebounds, and 1.5 blocks in 23.9 minutes per game in his freshman year at Arizona in 2001–02, starting 25 of 34 games. He continued to improve as a sophomore when he averaged 12.6 points, 8.0 rebounds, and 1.9 blocks in 25.4 minutes per game.

The accolades and expectations for Frye kept piling up when he earned first-team All-Pac-10 and USBWA All-District 9 Team honors as a junior. In 30 games he averaged 15.9 points, 7.4 rebounds, 1.9 assists, and 2.1 blocks in 30.3 minutes per game.

He could have easily left college after his sophomore and junior seasons and still been a lottery pick, but he wanted to play and start all four years.

As a senior, it became clear that his decision to stay in school was the correct one, as things just kept improving for him when received the University of Arizona's Sapphire Award, which is given to the outstanding senior male student-athlete. He also earned the 2004–05 Pacific-10 Conference Sportsmanship Award. For a second consecutive year, he earned First-Team All-Pac-10 and USBWA All-District 9 Team honors, as well as First-Team NABC All-NCAA District 15 selection. He averaged 15.8 points, 7.6 rebounds, 1.9 assists, and 2.3 blocks in 31.0 minutes per game. He would go down as one of the greatest players ever to play his collegiate ball for the famed University of Arizona.

Frye was selected with the eighth overall pick in the 2005 NBA draft by the New York Knicks. It was a draft that saw several big names selected ahead of him, including Andrew Bogut with the top pick by the Milwaukee Bucks. Deron Williams was taken third by the Utah Jazz, and, most notably, Chris Paul was selected fourth by the New Orleans Hornets. Frye had a solid rookie campaign and was selected to the 2005–06 NBA All-Rookie First Team, and he finished fifth in the Rookie of the Year voting.

His time in New York would be short: after only two seasons with the Knicks, he was traded along with Steve Francis to the Portland Trail Blazers in exchange for Zach Randolph, Fred Jones, and Dan Dickau. Frye would last only two underachieving years in Portland before he signed a reported two-year, $3.8 million contract with an option on the second year contract with the Phoenix Suns on July 14, 2009. Despite his height, he still possessed a dangerous outside game. During his first season with the Suns he was selected to the NBA All-Star Weekend Three-Point

Shootout. The Suns liked what they saw out of Frye in his first season with them and signed him to a new five-year, $30 million contract on July 8, 2010.

The next two seasons saw him reach career highs in points and other categories, and it looked as though his career would finally reach the potential many saw of him coming out of college. Just when his career was starting to peak, Frye learned he had an enlarged heart due to dilated cardiomyopathy, forcing him to sit out the entire 2012–13 season in the prime of his career.

He returned for the 2013–14 season but wasn't the player he was before sitting out the prior season. On June 23, 2014, Frye opted out of the final year of his contract with the Suns and signed a reported four-year, $32 million contract with the Orlando Magic. Unfortunely, his first season with the Magic was a bust, as he averaged his lowest point and rebound totals since his final season in Portland.

It was time for a change, and the Cavaliers hoped that he would bring his outside shot with him to Cleveland. Losing Andy wasn't risky considering the solid seasons Love and Thompson were having and his high probability of getting injured. If Frye could provide any spark off the bench, it would be worth the risk. Varejao was cut almost immediately by Portland and within hours signed on with the Golden State Warriors.

Following the trade, it only took a few wins until things seemed to be getting back to normal for Cleveland, as they were about to have a nice restful three days off before their Friday night showdown when the Washington Wizards would be coming to town. As usual, the Cavaliers could not go three days off without some type of drama, so once again things got strange. It all started when Stephen A. Smith reported that Kyrie Irving was unhappy in Cleveland. The often controversial ESPN mouthpiece had this to say: "Dating back to last year, I've been told that Kyrie

Irving ain't too happy being in Cleveland. The situation is not ideal for him. I don't know the particulars; I haven't spoken to him personally. It's something that I've been hearing for months; that under ideal circumstances he would prefer to be someplace other than Cleveland."

Smith would not reveal his sources or back it up with any facts. Before Cleveland fans had too much time to worry about that controversy, they were given something else to worry about the next day when LeBron James flew down to Miami to practice with his good friend and former teammate Dwyane Wade. Normally this type of thing wouldn't be that big of a deal, but on the heels of a recent losing streak combined with rumors of Irving being unhappy, the timing couldn't have been worse. LeBron didn't shy away from it or even try to hide it; in fact, he went out of his way to flaunt it by having his trainer tweet out a video of the practice session.

LeBron couldn't decide if he wanted to be loved by fans, or seen as a loner who just wanted to do his own thing and didn't care what people thought; it seemed to change daily with him. James may have said one thing in his letter when he came back to Cleveland, but he hadn't done much to live up to his words.

James compounded the problem the next day with a series of tweets. To explain his practice with Wade, he tweeted, "Can't replace great friends that reciprocate the same energy back to you in all facets of life," basically saying that he had true friends in Miami and he didn't have that bond with anyone back in Cleveland. A day earlier he had tweeted, "It's ok to know you've made a mistake. Cause we all do at times. Just be ready to live with whatever that comes with it and be with those who will protect you at all costs."

He seemed to love the drama and making everyone nervous when he continued to tweet cryptic messages later in the week, almost as if he were indicating it wouldn't be much longer until he left Cleveland again. "Do not take his greatness or anyone for granted!" was a clear message to Cleveland fans that if they continued to question him, he would have no bones about leaving them once again. As for those issues of team chemistry, James tweeted, "It's this simple. U can't accomplish the dream if everyone isn't dreaming the same thing everyday. Nightmares follow."

Perhaps James was referring to Kevin Love, who had just signed a deal to be the spokesman for Banana Republic. James, who has multiple endorsement deals himself, was upset that Love had lined one up instead of focusing on the team. It seemed just a tad bit hypocritical on the part of the self-professed King. Just when things seemed like they couldn't get any stranger, they did when coach Tyronn Lue gave Kevin Love the night off when the Cavaliers returned to the hardwood on Friday, March 4, against the visiting Washington Wizards. It seemed odd that Love would get the night off, since the team had just had three days off in a row. Perhaps it was a not-so-subtle way of Lue voicing his displeasure with Love, or secretly taking instructions from James. Both scenarios seemed likely.

The Wizards had embarrassed the Cavaliers less than a week earlier, and Cleveland was out for revenge. Despite being short-handed with Love on the bench, the Cavaliers looked well rested and hungry in a 108–83 rout. The 25-point win was impressive and a statement game. They followed it up the next night with Love back in the lineup, as they defeated the visiting Boston Celtics, 120–103. The Celtics gave them trouble in the first half, but a furious second-half rally put away the men in green.

It seemed as though they were putting the distractions behind them and were playing well until they traveled to sunny Florida for a pair of weekend games against the Orlando Magic and Miami Heat on consecutive nights. What would come of it was more of the frustrating basketball that kept Cleveland fans scratching their heads. After a lackluster 109–103 victory over Orlando, a team that they crushed three times previously under David Blatt, they barely showed up the following night in another blowout loss to the Miami Heat. The outcome was never in doubt, as the Heat dominated all night.

Even more concerning then the 122–101 loss was the way LeBron James could be seen all game joking around and smiling with his former teammate Dwyane Wade. He didn't seem to care, and it was evident to his teammates who were not happy with their leader's demeanor. Two days later, LeBron would refuse to speak with the Cleveland media before that Monday's shootaround back at home before their game with the Denver Nuggets. Their Jekyll and Hyde approach continued as the Toronto Raptors closed in on the number one spot in the East.

What had been a foregone conclusion that Cleveland would roll through the East and a finals meeting with the Golden State Warriors or San Antonio Spurs no longer appeared to be a sure thing if they didn't start playing better defense and stop looking too far ahead. For the first time all season, the Cavaliers were in real trouble if they didn't wake up fast.

Cleveland had struggled with back-to-back games all season long and would have an opportunity to turn that around, this time at home, as the Milwaukee Bucks and Brooklyn Nets were on the schedule on the following Wednesday and Thursday nights. It would be interesting to see what type of effort the Cavaliers decided to put forth against two inferior opponents.

Before they could focus on basketball, James took it upon himself to continue his bizarre comments and actions that had everyone including his own teammates and coaches questioning them. His first decision was to start ignoring the media and cutting them off from his social media accounts. It didn't stop there, as he went on to stop following the Cleveland Cavaliers on his social media accounts, as well. He purposely made a scene out of disrespecting his employer, blew off the local media with a response of "Next question" when they asked him about it, and then walked away from them completely.

Just when it seemed like he couldn't do anything else to get everyone upset and uneasy, he broke his media silence only long enough to let everyone know that it was his dream to play on the same team as Chris Paul, Carmelo Anthony, and Dwyane Wade and that he would even take a pay cut to do so. With the age of the superstars he named, along with the current salary cap being what it was, it was clear that the formation of his dream team would have to take place somewhere other than Cleveland. Not only did the comment shake up the fans, but also his teammates, as they began to wonder why he wasn't content simply playing with them. While the Cleveland coaching staff and rabid fan base wanted to focus solely on improving and hitting the playoffs at full stride, LeBron seemed focused on making them uneasy.

As the playoffs drew closer, the Cavaliers still looked like the best team in the Eastern Conference. However, every time they would seemingly get things turned around on the court, they would encounter more drama off of it. The next distraction focused on Kyrie Irving's romantic relationship with pop singer Kehlani Parrish. The R&B singer PartyNextDoor posted a since-deleted photo on Instagram that appeared to show himself and Parrish lying together in a bed. Kehlani had been romantically linked to Irving in the past, and later she posted another since-deleted photo implying that she attempted suicide.

Irving, in a series of tweets, addressed the situation and said he and Parrish were not dating at the time the initial photo was posted. He offered positive thoughts for Parrish and her family. "It's been hard to see what's been going on and not address the truth," Irving wrote. "I do not justify the picture or what dude did to try and spark all of this non sense that could have been avoided, but me and Kehlani were not dating when the picture came out. It's unfortunate that it's received so much attention but its become bigger because of a post that was misunderstood. Nothing but love and compassion over this way for her and her family. My only focus the Game I love to play every night," wrote Irving.

Heading into the last week of the season, Cleveland was 56–24, and the Toronto Raptors were 54–26. Cleveland held a two-game lead with two games to play, with Toronto holding the tiebreaker by winning the season series, two games to one. The Cavaliers just needed that one more win to clinch the top overall seed in the East, and they finally got it on April 11 against the Atlanta Hawks, 109–94, at Quicken Loans Arena.

LeBron finished up the season playing some of the best basketball he had in years, which was a very positive sign for Cleveland. He was the team's scoring leader with 25.3 points per game and also led the team with 6.8 assists. He proved he could still be physical with an average of 7.4 rebounds a game and once again showed his durability by playing in 76 of the 82 games. The Cavaliers went 1-5 without him, which made everyone nervous.

A lot of eyes were on Kyrie Irving, who was returning from a serious injury. He managed to make it back and stay healthy enough to play in 53 games. He was streaky at times and never seemed to be all the way back to his normal self, but he still averaged a solid 19.6 points and 4.7 assists.

As for the third member of the Big Three, when Kevin Love wasn't busy modeling Banana Republic shorts, he was pulling down a team-leading 9.9 rebounds a contest. His scoring average once again dropped to 16 points a game. Much like Irving, the most important stat for Love was games played, and he appeared in 77 of them. That was another great sign that he would be healthy heading into the playoffs and be that third scoring threat they needed to have. He would have to step it up in every area in the playoffs if the Cavaliers were going to have chance at going deep, let alone winning it all.

Tristan Thompson faced a great deal of pressure following his signing of a massive contract after his long holdout, and for the most part, he didn't live up to it. He was given the contract due to his stellar postseason play in 2015, as well as the team's concerns about Love's health. Thompson's durability held up, as he once again appeared in all 82 games. He averaged nine rebounds and just 7.8 points a game, the lowest scoring output of his career. Thompson would be judged harshly if he couldn't find a way to turn it on again for the upcoming playoffs.

One giant concern for the Cavaliers was that they didn't have a single player who averaged double digits in rebounds, or a single player who averaged double digits in assists. They had losing or .500 records against the Miami Heat, Indiana Pacers, Detroit Pistons, and Toronto Raptors, teams they could expect to see in the playoffs. This was not shaping up to be the cakewalk many thought it would be heading into the season. The most questioned move was the firing of head coach David Blatt when the team had the best record in the Eastern Conference. A move summed up by general manager David Griffin as "a lack of fit with our personnel and our vision" as the reason for Blatt's firing. His replacement, Tyronn Lue, led the team to a 27–14 in his tenure to finish the season. None of it would matter or be remembered if they could win it all, and the challenge awaited them.

CHAPTER 7

Sixteen Wins to Glory

THE PLAYOFFS FINALLY ARRIVED ON Sunday, April 17, after a season of struggle, drama, and controversy. The Cavs finished the regular season with the Eastern Conference's best record at 57–25 but never quite seemed like the favorites to win anything. They were constantly fighting questions, injuries, coaching moves, and various issues. Yet, through it all, they just kept winning and now were only 16 wins away from ending one of the longest championship droughts in the history of sports.

The upstart 44-win Detroit Pistons would be the first team standing in their way. Detroit was led by former Orlando head coach Stan Van Gundy, who had already proven with the Magic that he knew the recipe to beat the Cavaliers in the playoffs. The Pistons had a threesome of players who could score points by the bucketful in Reggie Jackson, Tobias Harris, and Andre Drummond, who was also a monster on the boards, averaging 14.8 a game. He was a multi-talented player who could beat an opponent several different ways. The way to stop Drummond would be to bring him to the foul line as much as possible. He set the NBA's lowest all-time single-season free-throw shooting percentage record in 2015–16 with an awful 35.5 percent mark.

In order to beat them, the Cavs would need to move the ball around and keep the offense fluid and not stagnant. Detroit had power, and Cleveland would need to out-finesse them them as well as they could. Despite its being a 1 vs. 8-seed matchup, Detroit presented a serious challenge to the Cavaliers, having beaten them in two of their three meetings during the regular season.

The Cavaliers would have to remain focused and ignore the talk of the Golden State Warriors and their epic 73-win season, as tough as it was. The Warriors had blown out the Houston Rockets the day before, and the Cavaliers knew they couldn't match it, nor try; a win was a win and that's what they had to focus on as the Pistons entered their building.

If the Pistons were an eight seed, someone forgot to tell them: they came out and took it right to the Cavaliers, giving Cleveland all they could handle. The Pistons, not known for three-point shooting, made 10 of 16 in the first half and finished 15 of 29. The Pistons held a 58–53 lead at halftime and still led by seven points early in the fourth quarter as the upset loomed and Cleveland fans got nervous in their seats. The Cavaliers would finally wake up long enough to go on a run of their own, capped off by several three-pointers from the red-hot Kevin Love to battle back and tie the game. The game remained tied, 88–88, with a little over six minutes to go before Kevin Love and Kyrie Irving once again took over and helped the Cavs go on another run.

They would hold on for a 106–101 victory to take Game One of the series. The come-from-behind win was aided by two players who were hurt in the previous year's playoffs: Irving scored 31 points in his first postseason game since being injured during the

Finals and Love, who went down in the first round, added 28. Love was on fire from behind the arc, hitting on four of his eight attempts. James was his usual dominant self, with 22 points, 11 rebounds, and six assists. James, who has been in the playoffs 14 of his 16 years in the NBA, helped his team win Game One of the opening round for the fourteenth straight season.

The Pistons took a short flight home, since they had two full days off before Game Two of the series on Wednesday April 20. They made the series opener interesting but simply couldn't pull off the upset. Keeping it close gave them the confidence to come out strong again in Game Two, and they hung tough for two and half quarters before Cleveland exploded with a barrage of points to pull away, 107–90, to put the Pistons in a 0–2 hole. Cleveland hit 20 of 38 three-point attempts in the contest, a risky strategy that paid off this time.

Pistons rookie forward Stanley Johnson, who scored only nine points, spouted off after the game, saying he was in LeBron's head and making other questionable comments. It made little sense for Johnson to speak out after his team lost by 17 points with James scoring 27, and in the long run all it did was motivate the Cavaliers' entire roster.

Cleveland knew they would be in for a tough battle during Game Three in Detroit, as the Pistons would not want to go down three games to none. As tough as the Pistons played, the Cavaliers kept their heads in the game, ignored any off-court drama or dirty plays by Detroit, and came away with the win, 101–91.

Andre Drummond, who continued to struggle from the foul line after going a dreadful 4-for-16 in Game Two, decided to resort to playing dirty in Game Three in the hopes of throwing James and the Cavaliers off. Drummond threw two nasty elbows at LeBron during the game, the second half one resulting in a technical foul. But James and the rest of the team kept their cool and pulled away late to win it.

Down by nine in the fourth, Detroit went on an 8–0 run, forcing the Cavs to call a timeout. Irving responded with a three-pointer, and J. R. Smith later added one of his own to make it 95–90. The final dagger came from Kyrie Irving, who hit a fade-away three with less than a second on the shot clock to put the Cavaliers up by eight and end all doubt with 43 seconds to go. James and Love scored 20 points apiece. Drummond hit only one of six free throws, and Van Gundy took him out with 6:02 remaining to prevent Cleveland from intentionally fouling him. Even in the last two minutes—when those intentional off-the-ball fouls are illegal—Van Gundy kept him on the bench.

Three games into their second postseason together, the Cavaliers were finally showing everyone just how dangerous they could be when the Big Three were all healthy and rolling at the same time.

The Detroit Pistons were the dominant team in the Eastern Conference during the early part of LeBron James's career. They won the NBA championship his rookie year and lost in the finals the following season. In 2006, the Cavs nearly stunned them by forcing a dramatic seven-game series in the second round of the playoffs before ultimately falling to them. The next year the Cavs would not be denied and toppled them in the Eastern Conference Finals on the strength of a 48-point explosion by James in a double overtime Game Five at the Palace, followed by a rookie named Daniel "Boobie" Gibson going off from three-ball land to close the series out in front of a packed house at Quicken Loans Arena.

It was such a gigantic upset that almost no one saw it coming. It was LeBron's coming-out party, and many around the league believed it was the first step to leading the Cavaliers into the promised land and beginning a dynasty of their own. But they were swept by the San Antonio Spurs in the 2007 NBA Finals, and LeBron and that group would never return. Fast-forward nearly ten years later and the roles were much different, the mighty Cavaliers a heavy favorite to close out the Pistons and move on to the conference semifinals. So much had changed, but in some ways, so little.

Sure, LeBron had gone to Miami and won multiple titles, but in a way, it seemed as though he never got over the hump, the hump being a title win in Cleveland, his hometown and the city he promised it to. The situation was still very similar based on the pressure remaining to win it all, and once again having to go through Detroit on his path. The only difference was this time the Pistons were the first roadblock, and not the last, on their way to the NBA Finals. In the end, it was one of James's teammates who helped finish the clean sweep of the Pistons. So many times in his early years with the Cavs he would fall short because he didn't have the proper help. This time he did, and Kyrie Irving made sure of it.

Irving nailed a huge three late in the fourth quarter, then made a stellar defensive stop in the final seconds as Reggie Jackson took a desperation three-point shot from 26 feet out to try and win it but barely missed, giving Cleveland the 100–98 win. Jackson begged the ref for a foul call on Irving, but it wasn't even close. Ten years after losing to the Pistons in a memorable series, the Cavaliers were moving on, and just as they did then, they felt it was now or never.

The Atlanta Hawks had been the best regular-season team in the Eastern Conference a year earlier, but things were much different twelve months later when they once again faced Cleveland in the postseason. The biggest difference this season was that the Cavaliers held the higher seed (1) against the Hawks (4). The still-dangerous Hawks were coming off of a six-game opening-round series win against the pesky Boston Celtics. They would have revenge on their mind from Cleveland's sweep in the 2015 NBA Eastern Conference Finals.

The Hawks boasted the sharpshooting backcourt combination of Jeff Teague and Kyle Korver, both of whom showed how dangerous they could be when feeling the shooter's touch on any given night. Korver was a knock-down threat from long range as the owner of the NBA record for the highest three-point field goal percentage (53.6 percent) for a season. At one point in his career, he held the NBA record for most consecutive games with a made three-pointer (127).

Korver's backcourt teammate Jeff Teague earned an NBA All-Star bid in 2015 and was having another solid season, averaging 15.7 points and 5.9 assists per game. He was a huge reason the Hawks were back in the playoffs and doing well.

Mix in fellow starters Al Horford, Paul Millsap, and defensive specialist Kent Bazemore, and it was clear why the Hawks had returned to the playoffs. They weren't nearly as good as the prior year, but the Cavaliers knew they couldn't take them for granted despite the prior season's sweep as the lower seed.

By the time Monday, May 2, 2016, rolled around, the Cavaliers hadn't played in eight days and everyone expected them to be rusty. They weren't and instead came out sharp in Game One at home to build an 18-point second-half lead. Behind some furious shooting from Millsap and Dennis Schroder (who finished with 27 points), the Hawks came back in the second half and actually took a one-point lead. Coach Lue wouldn't allow his team to lose its composure despite several hard fouls by Atlanta that weren't called, and the Cavaliers would regain control to win Game One, 104–93, despite LeBron James and Kyrie Irving only getting to the foul line a combined three times in the entire game, all in the fourth quarter.

The Cavaliers didn't get the calls in Game One but remained focused on the prize and beat the Hawks for the ninth straight time in the playoffs. They wouldn't need any calls in Game Two, as it was over before the Hawks even realized what happened. The Cavaliers came out and blitzed the Hawks by making 18 three-pointers in the first half to put the game away. As the half-time show went on, the Hawks were still trying to pick their jaws up off the ground, with the Cavaliers leading, 74–38, in one of the most impressive first-half performances in NBA history. By the time the slaughter was over, the Cavaliers won, 123–98, on the strength of an NBA-record 25 three-pointers. They also broke the postseason record of 21 set by Golden State only a week earlier. Cleveland finished 25 of 45 from behind the arc and had ten players make at least one three-pointer. The main assassin was J. R. Smith with seven three-point shots made, six of which came in the first half. The Atlanta Hawks' Twitter account even got in on the action and couldn't shy away from the embarrassment, tweeting during the game at one point, "Enough with the corner Three's." They would go on to tweet as the game got more out of hand, "If you take away their three's, we are right in this."

It was a milestone night for LeBron James, as he passed Tim Duncan to move into fifth place on the all-time playoff scoring list and played in his 184th postseason game, tying him with Celtics great Robert Parish for 13th place. The Cavaliers were serving notice that they were healthy, confident, and rolling at the perfect time.

Not everyone was impressed by Cleveland's three-point barrage, and it didn't take long for someone to say something foolish, as Charles Barkley uttered some truly idiotic thoughts following the game during the TNT postgame show. He mentioned how the Hawks should have been embarrassed to the point that they needed "to take someone out" from the Cavaliers. Basically, Sir Charles was saying that the Cavaliers deserved to have someone hurt. It was hardly a comment that Cleveland fans took lightly, considering that *exact thing* happened to Kevin Love a year earlier. Barkley's comments were the talk of the NBA instead of the impressive win by Cleveland. It was a shame that a guy who didn't even compete in the game took home some of the headlines from it.

For Charles Barkley, this was just one of many on- and off-the-court incidents that had people questioning his judgment and personal conduct, despite his immense talent. In March 1991, during a game in New Jersey, Barkley attempted to spit on a fan who had been heckling him with racial slurs; however, it landed on a young girl nearby. He would be penalized without pay and fined $10,000 for spitting and using abusive language at the fan.

Sir Charles often said he wasn't a role model and even went as far as to shoot a Nike commercial with that catchphrase. He also released this statement: "I think the media demands that athletes be role models because there's some jealousy involved. It's as if they say, this is a young black kid playing a game for a living and making all this money, so we're going to make it tough on him. And what they're really doing is telling kids to look up to someone they can't become, because not many people can be like we are. Kids can't be like Michael Jordan."

His actions would continue to back up his words when he was arrested for breaking a man's nose during a fight after a game with the Milwaukee Bucks and also for throwing a man through a plate-glass window after being struck with a glass of ice. His comments about having a Hawks player hurt a Cavaliers player, sadly, weren't surprising. Cleveland simply had to hope that no one on the Hawks would heed them.

When the Cavaliers traded longtime fan favorite Anderson Varejao back in February, many fans were upset and couldn't understand the logic. He had been through so much with the city and team, only to be cast aside for Channing Frye.

While Andy was seen as a regular member of the community and someone who had become the face of Cleveland sports during some very thin times, Frye was the new guy on the block and still a relative stranger to fans. This didn't mean he was a bad guy; far from it, as in 2007, Frye established the Channing Frye Foundation. It was founded with the goal of pointing youth in a positive and healthy direction. In 2010, Frye and his wife established the Frye Family Foundation in order to give back to the communities that are important to them, in particular, Portland, Oregon, and Phoenix, Arizona. Frye also sponsors a charity kickball tournament in Portland. He was actually a great guy, but one the Cavalier fans simply didn't get behind because he was seen as the guy who replaced Andy.

All that would change in Game Three, as Frye helped the Cavaliers go up 3–0 with 27 points on 10 of 13 shooting, including 7 of 9 from three-point range, in a thrilling, come-from-behind 121–108 win at Philips Arena. His seven three-pointers were part of a fantastic shooting night that saw Cleveland sink 21 total three-pointers, only four shy of the record they set less than 48 hours earlier. Channing Frye had arrived, and Cleveland fans were happy to have him.

It was a battle all night, as the Hawks used a 22–7 run late in the second quarter to take a 63–55 lead into halftime. Atlanta remained in control throughout the third quarter and took a six-point lead into the fourth quarter.

The Cavaliers would explode in the fourth quarter, outscoring the Hawks, 36–17, to go up 3–0 in the series. They were on fire and couldn't miss, played great defense, and continued to shut down Atlanta when it counted. It was a total team effort and showed once again that when Cleveland was rolling on all cylinders, they were hard to beat.

Two nights after setting the NBA record with 25 three-pointers, the Cavaliers were nearly as good in a 21-of-39 performance that moved them within one victory of their second consecutive playoff sweep over the Hawks. Not only was Frye on target, the rest of the team was cruising, as well, as James and Irving each scored 24 points, while Love chipped in with 21. The team showed a massive amount of heart after being down by 11 at one point, and Kevin Love even showed some emotion when he became irate at several bad calls. His teammates calmed him down and then went to work righting the wrong.

It was pure domination when it counted the most, with Cleveland scoring 22 of the game's final 27 points and the Hawks making just two of their final 12 shots, with four turnovers mixed in. Frustrated from blowing the lead, and seeing the seconds wind down on another loss, Jeff Teague apparently took some of Charles Barkley's advice. As James attempted to drive to the basket in the closing seconds, Teague shoved him into the seats behind the basket with a shoulder shot, drawing a flagrant foul. It was much too little, too late, and the Cavaliers were on the brink of going back into the Eastern Conference finals.

The Cavaliers showed pure hustle and heart off the boards, outrebounding the Hawks by a 55–28 margin. Love had 15 rebounds, while James and Tristan Thompson grabbed 13 apiece. Nobody on the Hawks had more than eight. Past Cavalier teams might have folded under the pressure after falling behind, but this one was different, and the best was yet to come.

Game Four would come down to the wire, but thanks to a stellar 27-point effort from Kevin Love, the Cavaliers put the Hawks away, 100–99. Atlanta had a chance to score the last bucket, but James tied up Dennis Schroder with 2.8 seconds to go, allowing Cleveland to advance. The question was, who was next?

CHAPTER 8

The Great White North

ENTERING THE 2015–16 SEASON, THE Toronto Raptors had been in the NBA for twenty seasons; boasted such all stars as Vince Carter, Tracy McGrady, Chris Bosh, Marcus Camby, Damon Stoudamire, and Andrea Bargnani in their history; and yet had only advanced past the first round of the playoffs once. This season would be different: for the first time in franchise history, they had seemed to put it all together in reaching the Eastern Conference finals.

Toronto was finally able to get over that hump thanks to great coaching by Dwane Casey. He had struggled in his prior coaching gig as the head man in Minnesota from 2005 to 2007. He got a second chance, this time with the Raptors in 2011, and took full advantage. Under his tutelage, the young Raptors improved each season and in 2015–16 recorded a franchise-record 56 wins, securing the second overall seed in the Eastern Conference.

One big reason for their improvement was free agent pickup DeMarre Carroll, who signed a four-year deal for 60 million dollars after coming over from the Atlanta Hawks to be their defensive backbone. He was great when he played, but injuries limited him to just 26 regular-season games.

On December 7, he was ruled out indefinitely with a bruised right knee. He would miss nine straight games with the injury, returning to action on December 26 against the Milwaukee Bucks. He managed to play in just five more games before the same knee forced him to sit out the team's January 4 loss to the Cleveland Cavaliers. Two days later, he underwent surgery on his right knee and would miss the next 41 games. The Raptors would need Carroll to stay healthy if they were going to have any chance at stopping Cleveland.

While Carroll was counted on to play defense, the Raptors got most of their offense from a stellar one-two scoring punch of guards Kyle Lowry and DeMar DeRozan. They formed one of the best backcourts in the league and were a key reason the Raptors had reached the conference finals.

In his tenth NBA season out of Villanova and fourth with the Raptors, Lowry was averaging a career-high 21.2 points a game. He also averaged 6.4 assists and 2.1 steals a game, to become the total package.

His backcourt mate DeRozan was every bit as dangerous in his seventh year out of USC. He had played his entire career with the Raptors and improved every season with the team, with his scoring average increasing from 8.6 to 23.5. Both were named All-Stars in 2016; and Cavs point guard Kyrie Irving, who was left off the team, was anxious to show everyone how much of a mistake that was.

Working against the Raptors would be the absence of starting center Jonas Valančiūnas. Playing in his fourth NBA season, the Lithuanian had emerged as one of the best big men in the league but suffered a sprained ankle during the previous playoff series with Miami and was ruled out for at least the first two games of this series, if not longer. It was a big blow to Toronto's hopes of advancing, since he was having a terrific postseason before getting hurt. In Game One of the Raptors' first round playoff series against the seventh-seeded Indiana Pacers, Valančiūnas set a franchise playoff record with 19 rebounds, surpassing his own mark set in 2014. He would continue to impress in Game Two, recording a playoff career-high 23 points and 15 rebounds in a 98–87 win.

As for Cleveland, things seemed eerily similar to the 2009 postseason, when they had also swept through Detroit and Atlanta in eight games to start the postseason. They were a heavy favorite to beat the Magic in '09, when everyone was already looking ahead to a LeBron James vs. Kobe Bryant matchup in the finals. This year carried the same expectations, since everyone was anticipating the LeBron James vs. Stephen Curry rematch in the finals.

Seven years earlier, they were guilty of looking past Orlando, and they were stung because of it, getting bounced from the playoffs by the Magic in six games. The Cavaliers were determined not to let it happen again in 2016 and jumped out to a 66–44 halftime lead in the opener. Cleveland outscored the Raptors 33–16 in the second quarter, going on a 20–2 run at one point. It should be noted that in Game One of the Orlando series in '09, they held a large halftime lead, only to blow it and lose the game. The difference now was they were more talented, better focused, and well coached. Unlike '09, the Cavaliers didn't allow the Raptors to get back into Game One and ended up blowing them out, 115–84.

It was total domination, as they were able to sit LeBron James and other starters after three quarters. James connected on his first nine shots, on the way to going 11 of 13 in a 24-point effort, while Kyrie Irving led all scorers with 27 along with five assists. Cleveland shot 67 percent in the first half, and 55 percent for the game.

The 31-point victory was a team playoff record. They cooled off from three-point range, only making 7 of 20 attempts, but they didn't need the outside attack because they dominated the paint.

The Cavaliers defense knew that locking down Kyle Lowry was crucial, and they did just that in Game One. He was held to just eight points after he had scored 35 points in the series-clinching win against Miami two days earlier. DeMar DeRozan was one of the few bright spots for Toronto, putting in 18 points, but it was not nearly enough. The blowout win also allowed the Cavaliers to rest James, who would only play 28 minutes and spend the entire fourth quarter resting on the bench.

Cleveland's defense was not only strong, but also clean, as DeRozan and Lowry did not attempt a free throw the entire game. It was a whopping stat that told the story. Another important stat was the Cavaliers outrebounding the Raptors, 45–23. The nine-game winning streak to start the playoffs was the longest in franchise history. Game One belonged to Cleveland, and if the Raptors didn't wake up soon, so would the series.

The biggest difference between this Cavaliers team and the squads during LeBron's first tenure was that the prior ones always felt like underdogs. They were always trying to get past Detroit, and later Boston. They were never the team everyone expected to roll through the playoffs and right to a NBA title. After their Game Two victory at Quicken Loans Arena, 108–89, it was starting to feel that way. Cleveland had now won ten in a row to start the postseason, and since LeBron James's return, they had gone 22–2 and had won their last 17 games against the Eastern Conference in the playoffs dating back to the 2015 run. The Cavaliers were only the fourth team in NBA history to start the playoffs at 10–0, joining the 1989 Lakers, 2001 Lakers, and 2012 San Antonio Spurs. Only one of the three teams went on to win the NBA championship, however, so it was a far from a sure thing that the hot start would result in a title and end the fifty-two-year championship drought in Cleveland.

A few days earlier, ESPN premiered a documentary titled *Believeland* that focused on all of the sports misery in Cleveland history, a subject done to death and of no relevance to the current state of Cleveland sports, but the national sports powerhouse network never missed a chance for a dig. In a way, it seemed like perhaps the film about the "Cleveland curse" may have been just what the city needed to break it. Shortly following the film's conclusion, Cleveland native Stipe Miocic won the UFC Heavyweight title in Brazil against champion Fabricio Werdum.

Stipe wasn't the only one to help with the mojo, as the Indians proceeded to win five straight games against the Reds and Red Sox. The Cleveland Gladiators indoor football team of the AFL did their part, as well, as they also won that Monday night in double-overtime. The AHL Lake Erie Monsters also joined the fun by advancing to the Western Conference finals and were only eight wins away from winning the Calder Cup. It wasn't just the Cavaliers feeling the resurgence, it was the entire city!

A big reason for Cleveland's 2–0 series lead was the continued stellar play of LeBron James, who had a triple-double in Game Two with 23 points, 11 rebounds, and 11 assists. Unlike previous seasons, most recently last year, LeBron didn't have to do it himself because this time he had plenty of support from his teammates: Kyrie Irving went off for 26 points while Kevin Love chipped in with 19. The first two games weren't even close, with Cleveland winning by a combined 50 points, and it would have been more than that had they not pulled their starters in the fourth quarter of both games.

Despite the controversy and second-guessing that came with Tyronn Lue replacing head coach David Blatt when the team was in first place halfway through the year, the rookie coach's postseason performance was slowly starting to quiet down the doubters when he passed the legendary Pat Riley for the most consecutive playoff wins to begin a coaching career.

Perhaps the biggest reason that Lue was successful where Blatt struggled was that Lue never hesitated to correct a player regardless of his stature on the team. Rumor had it that Blatt was afraid to correct any of the Big Three, and because of that the team suffered and it caused several rifts. A story leaked out between Games Two and Three that earlier in the year, Lue actually told James to "shut the fuck up and let me coach, I got this" during a timeout, and that was the turning point for the team. It was also rumored that Lue was very upset with James for pandering to his former Heat teammates and friends during their last trip there, and that he had set James straight after that, as well. Whatever he did, whatever he said, it sure was working.

Perhaps the biggest improvement as a result of the coaching change was felt by Kevin Love, who was finally playing with the aggressiveness and scoring ability they expected when they traded for him. In Minnesota, Love was one of the best players in the entire NBA, the type of scoring machine who was an offensive threat all by himself. Blatt never seemed interested in having him do much of anything other than spot up along the perimeter, and with that went Love's confidence and overall effectiveness.

According to Dave McMenamin of ESPN, Lue was so eager to get through to Love and get him going that he actually told him, "Kevin, you got to be more aggressive. Tell LeBron, 'I'm a bad motherfucker, too, so throw me the ball.'" Love responded by averaging 18.9 points and 12.5 rebounds through the first two rounds.

Not only were the Cavaliers winning, but they were getting in the heads of the Raptors, as well. Lowry, who was stuggling, left the bench after coming out of the game with 2:35 remaining in the second quarter to blow off some steam with the Cavs in the middle of a 16–2 run.

Raptors head coach Dwane Casey was confident that his team would climb back in the series as he addressed the media with these comments following Game Two: "I don't think our guys have quit. I refuse to believe that. We've won 56 [regular-season] games. We've been down before. We've had some rough patches and we've bounced back. I think this is the first time in the play-offs we've lost two games in a row, so this team will bounce back. I believe in them and they've got to believe in themselves, and I think they do."

Casey's confidence in his team was well founded, as the Raptors bounced back by winning Game Three in Toronto with a dominant 99–84 blowout win. Kevin Love had the worst post-season performance of his career with only three points on 1 of 9 shooting. Kyrie Irving wasn't much better, going 3 of 19 from the field for a paltry 13 points. DeRozan and Lowry awoke from their slumber, with DeRozan scoring 32 points while Lowry put in 20. Perhaps the biggest reason the Cavaliers dropped their first game of the playoffs was their inability to box out Bismack Biyombo, who yanked down an incredible 26 rebounds, a Raptors playoff record. He had a total of only nine in the first two games.

Game Four was a wild one, as it saw the Raptors build a second-half lead of 18 points, only to watch LeBron and the Cavaliers climb back into it in the fourth, even going up by three with six minutes remaining. Behind the scoring machine back-court of Lowry and DeRozan, along with the amazing rebound-ing skills of Biyombo, the Raptors would come back for a 105–99 win to even the series.

Once again, it was a combination of Kevin Love being a nonfactor, J. R. Smith failing to play much defense, and both Lowry (35 points) and DeRozan (32) going off. Perhaps the biggest factor was the Cavaliers' inability to crash the boards, as Biyombo once again dominated the glass with 14 rebounds. It was the little-known Biyombo who was starting to make all the difference: he was only in there to replace an injured Jonas Valančiūnas, but he was the right man at the right time, and the Cavaliers couldn't seem to keep him off the boards.

To some extent, it wasn't a shock that the Cavaliers were struggling so much to stop the Raptors in Toronto, because the Raptors were a dominant home team all season. They went 32–9 during the regular season at the Air Canada Centre. There was only one team in the Eastern Conference with a better home record, and that was Cleveland, exactly where the series was headed back to for two of the final three games. The Cavaliers needed to capitalize.

Heading into Game Five, the Cavaliers finally said, "ENOUGH IS ENOUGH!" It was never close, as the Cavaliers ran roughshod over Toronto, 116–78. They led by as many as 43 points at one point, and the Raptors could not stop them. Not only was the offense clicking (Love scored 25, James 23, and Irving 23), but the defense finally stepped up. They picked up 11 steals, including four by J. R. Smith. They were able to box out Bismack Biyombo, limiting him him to only four rebounds.

It was incredible how much could change in less than three days. The Cavaliers hoped to carry that momentum with them when they traveled back up to the great white north for Game Six.

Cleveland was 0–4 in Toronto on the season, and the Raptors looked to keep their home record perfect against them while staying alive in the series. Lowry scored 35 points and Biyombo had nine rebounds and a block in 26 minutes, but despite those two impressive performances, Cleveland won in blowout fashion, 113–87. Cleveland was now set to advance to the NBA Finals for the second straight season. This would be the sixth straight trip for LeBron James dating back to his years with the Miami Heat.

Toronto scored 87 points as a team in Game Six, while Cleveland's Big Three of Love, James, and Irving tallied 83 by themselves. LeBron had 33 points and 11 rebounds. Irving had nine assists and three steals while scoring 30 points. Perhaps the most important stat line came from Kevin Love, who scored 20 points with 12 rebounds, showing once again that as he went, so went the team.

The Cavaliers had finally won in Toronto, and by doing so, they captured the third Eastern Conference championship in franchise history. The only question remained, who would they play? Two teams remained, and they both provided very intriguing and challenging matchups. The Oklahoma City Thunder had been the third seed in the West, and after defeating the heavily favored San Antonio Spurs, winners of 67 games, they took on the 73-win Golden State Warriors in the Western Conference Finals. After shocking the media and fans by going up three games to one in the series, the Thunder began to choke, losing two straight to even the series until Game Seven in Oakland saw the Warriors put them away for good with a 96–88 victory to advance to the NBA Finals and a rematch with the Cavaliers.

Cleveland and their fans still felt that had the Cavaliers had a healthy roster, they would have defeated Golden State in the previous season's Finals. Playing without Irving and Love had been too much to overcome.

If you think about how close the Cavaliers came without two of their three best players, this year's team had the talent to end Cleveland's fifty-two-year championship drought. OKC had come up short again, as Kevin Durant and Russell Westbrook had proven they are light years away from becoming a Jordan/Pippen-like duo.

On the other hand, the Warriors showed everyone once again just how good they are. Cleveland lost the season series with Golden State, 2–0. One loss came on Christmas day, with the other coming at home and leading to David Blatt's being fired. Cleveland's quest for revenge and a long-awaited championship was set to begin.

CHAPTER 9

The Comeback

PERHAPS IT WAS WRITTEN IN the stars for it to happen this way. In many ways it almost seemed too simple the first time around. A struggling basketball town in desperate search for a savior wins a magical lottery. The next thing you know, the "chosen one" from the hometown school of St. Vincent-St. Mary is drafted as the next big thing to bring Cleveland out of the doldrums. And sure enough, he did exactly that in his first tenure here.

LeBron James led the Cavs to multiple Eastern Conference finals and even one NBA Finals in his first stint. He won two regular season MVP awards, and it looked like they were on the cusp of winning it all several times before he left for South Beach. The day he made "The Decision" has forever since lived in infamy, and many Cleveland fans cringe at the thought of that ugly night.

Then, in the summer of 2014, a drama unfolded worthy of a Hollywood script, when the hometown boy found his redemption in the form of a beautiful letter to the fans announcing his return.

The results were felt immediately, as he led the Cavaliers back to the playoffs before his team was ravaged with injuries. They fought extremely hard and he played the best series of his life, the best series, some say, in all of NBA Finals history. But it simply wasn't enough, because it was the Golden State Warriors who celebrated on the hardwood in Cleveland. It had been less than a year since the Cleveland fans lived through that nightmare, and the thirst for revenge was strong.

The last time Cleveland won a major sporting world championship was back in 1964, when the Browns claimed the National Football League title. It seemed unfathomable to think that the city had gone over fifty years without winning another one. The trophy case in Cleveland had gone dusty and lonely.

In the 1980s, Cleveland fans had to suffer through a last-second drive and a goal-line fumble in consecutive seasons that kept the Browns from reaching the Super Bowl. Their beloved football team would eventually relocate to Baltimore in 1995 in a move that seemed surreal and felt like a really bad dream as opposed to harsh, cold reality. The expansion team that replaced them in 1999 has reached the postseason just once.

Baseball fans watched as their precious Tribe, a team so steeped in tradition and heart, fell just short of a World Series title in 1997 as they crumpled in extra innings of a Game Seven they had control of until the bottom of the ninth. Would the Cavs be the team to finally stop the curse? It was their third NBA Finals appearance in 46 seasons. They were swept by the San Antonio Spurs dynasty in '07 and gave the Warriors everything they could handle in 2015.

Perhaps the tides were finally turning in the summer of 2016. It wasn't just the Cavs, but the entire city of Cleveland that had been on the rise. The Republican National Convention would take place at the Quicken Loans Arena in mid-July. The Lake

Erie Monsters were on the doorstep of winning the American Hockey League's Calder Cup Championship. MMA fighter Stipe Miocic, a Cleveland native, had recently become the UFC world heavyweight champion. Even Hollywood was getting in on the act, as the next *The Fast and the Furious* movie was being filmed minutes from the Quicken Loans Arena. Cleveland was suddenly the place to be, and the Cavaliers' winning a championship would be the cherry on the sundae.

Standing in their way was the Golden State Warriors, a team that proudly set the NBA single-season wins record with 73. They went 39–2 at home and would have the homecourt advantage in the finals for the second straight year. They had been left for dead just one week earlier when they trailed the OKC Thunder, three games to one, only to remind everyone just how good they were.

There were three important keys to beating the Warriors. The first would be shutting down their incredible three-point attack led by the "Splash Brothers," Klay Thompson and Stephen Curry, the winner of back-to-back league MVP awards. In the regular season alone, they combined to connect on a whopping 678 three-point field goals, an NBA record. Curry could do it all: he had the kind of shot that could put the dagger in any opposing team's momentum, and he could connect from anywhere on the floor. Thompson set a playoff record by hitting 11 three-pointers as part of his 41-point effort during the Game Six comeback against Oklahoma City. If the Cavaliers were unable to stop Golden State from hitting threes, then they would have to make their share of them. They proved in the Atlanta series they could do so when they set a playoff record by making 25 three-point shots in a game.

The second and most vital key, perhaps the biggest thing they were missing last year, was roster depth and a strong bench. Losing both Kevin Love and Kyrie Irving in 2015 forced J. R. Smith and

Matthew Dellavedova into unfamiliar roles and took them off the bench, where they were most effective. Now, with Channing Frye joining the likes of Smith, Delly, Richard Jefferson, and Timofey Mozgov, the Cavaliers were as deep as ever and a legitimate threat. A year earlier, the bench included Mike Miller, Joe Harris, Brendan Haywood, and Shawn Marion. To say this was a slight upgrade would be a gigantic understatement. The Cavaliers were now twelve deep and would need all twelve to compete with the Warriors.

Last but not least, in order to beat the Warriors, the Cavaliers would have to practice good ball movement and stay away from hero ball. The biggest problem they ran into last year was lack of depth and quality shooters, so it became a one-man gang with LeBron James. This year, things were different, and they needed to spread the ball out and get everyone into the mix to keep the Warriors guessing. Whether it was J. R. Smith, Tristan Thompson, or even Richard Jefferson, whoever stepped up as their pivotal fourth scorer behind James, Love, and Irving could make all the difference.

The Warriors were a team of destiny in their own right, and despite winning 73 games, they almost seemed like underdogs at times. When you factor in that most of their key players, with the exception of Andre Iguodala, were homegrown, it was hard not to root for the Warriors, because they did things the right way. They also sported three former Cavaliers players: Anderson Varejao, Shaun Livingston, and Marreese Speights.

Not only was their bench loaded with the likes of Livingston and Speights, it was someone who would be inserted into the starting lineup just for the finals alone who looked to make the major difference for the second consecutive year.

Andre Iguodala was largely credited as the difference maker when he replaced Andrew Bogut in the starting lineup after

Game Three with the Warriors down 2–1. The bold move to go small by coach Steve Kerr worked, and the Warriors were holding up the championship trophy three games later. Iguodala finished the series averaging 16.3 points, 4.0 assists, and 5.8 rebounds. It was enough to garner him the MVP of the series in a shock over both Curry and LeBron.

Andre Iguodala spent the first eight years of his career with the Philadelphia 76ers, and he served them well. He played in all 82 games in four of those seasons and led the team in several categories during that time. He was the face of 76ers basketball, averaging nearly 19 points, six assists, and two steals a game. He made it to the playoffs five times with the Sixers without making it past the first round.

While he was in Philly, Iguodala was a member of the United States national team in the 2010 FIBA World Championship, winning the gold medal. He was also selected for the 2012 Olympics team that competed in London, largely due to his exceptional defensive ability. He helped Team USA win the gold medal against Spain in a 107–100 victory.

It was a shock to 76ers fans when he was dealt to the Denver Nuggets in a series of trades also involving the Sixers, Los Angeles Lakers, and Orlando Magic two days before winning the gold medal. He wasn't the only big name in the deal, as other players involved included All-Stars Andrew Bynum and Dwight Howard. He only played one season in Denver before agreeing to a four-year, $48 million deal with the Warriors on July 5, 2013.

As with Shaun Livingston before him, it was the smartest move he could have made. While he was known for scoring big and flashy dunks in Philly, it was upon his arrival in Golden State that his defensive game really took off. In his first year with the Warriors, Iguodala was named to the All-NBA Defensive First Team. It was those skills that led Kerr to insert him into the starting lineup in the 2015 finals to try and contain LeBron James. He couldn't stop him completely, but he did a great job containing him, as James made only 38.1 percent of his shots when Iguodala was in the game, compared to 44 percent when he wasn't, and he was once again about to be served with that crucial task.

Iguodala became the first player to win the Finals MVP award without starting a game during the regular season. He was also the first to not have started every game in the finals.

Despite Iguodala's run as finals MVP, Kerr knew that he best served the team coming off the bench in the regular season; once again, Kerr was right, as Iguodala finished as runner-up for the 2015–16 NBA Sixth Man of the Year Award. Kerr also knew the best time to bring him off the bench and back into the starting rotation; this time it would be in place of Harrison Barnes in Game Seven, after his defensive work against Kevin Durant and Russell Westbrook was a key to the Warriors' winning Game Six.

Steve Kerr, the head coach of the Warriors, had a heartwarming story of his own. His 15-year playing career with the Suns, Cavs, Bulls, Magic, Blazers, and Spurs stretched from 1988 to 2003. He was a four-time NBA champion as a player, with the Bulls from 1996 to 1998 and in 2003 with the Spurs.

Kerr graduated from the University of Arizona in 1988 with a Bachelor of General Studies, with emphasis on history, sociology, and English. He was seen as one of the smartest players on every team he was on. He played with such stars as Michael Jordan, Mark Price, Scottie Pippen, Tim Duncan, Tony Parker, and David Robinson and for men like Phil Jackson and Gregg Popovich. He learned from the best.

After giving broadcasting a try, Kerr became general manager of the Phoenix Suns beginning with the 2007–08 season. He served until deciding it wasn't for him and stepped down as president and GM of the Suns on June 15, 2010. He resumed his broadcasting career, returning to his role as an analyst for Turner Sports.

On May 14, 2014, Kerr reached an agreement to become the head coach of the Golden State Warriors, succeeding Mark Jackson. It didn't take Kerr long to start installing the systems he had learned in his playing days, as he employed elements of the triangle offense from his playing days in Chicago under Phil Jackson, the spacing and pace of Gregg Popovich in San Antonio, and the uptempo principles Alvin Gentry used in Phoenix when Kerr was the GM.

Kerr fit into the role of coaching like a perfectly sculpted hand into a tailor-made glove. He became the first coach to start his career with a 21–2 record en route to an impressive 67-win season that saw him finish runner-up in the NBA Coach of the Year voting while he led Golden State to their first championship since 1975.

Kerr would not start the 2015–16 season with the Warriors; he took an indefinite leave of absence to rehabilitate his back, which had troubled him since the previous season's finals. Assistant coach Luke Walton assumed Kerr's duties, and the team didn't miss a beat, getting off to one of the hottest starts in NBA history. Kerr didn't return to the sidelines until January 22, 2016, missing 43 games. He was credited for the wins he wasn't on the sidelines for, and he became the first person in NBA history to be a part of 70-win teams as a player and head coach. He was also was named 2015–16 NBA Coach of the Year despite only coaching in half of the games. In his two seasons, he was 140–24, an impressive winning percentage of over 85 percent.

The Warriors had the NBA's best player and coach as voted on by NBA writers; it was now up to the Cavaliers to try and stop them. LeBron and the gang were not intimidated, and they were set to take it to them with a healthy roster and quality game plan when Game One tipped off Thursday June 2, 2016, at the Oracle Arena in Oakland, California.

The good news for Cleveland was that they held Curry to only 11 points, and Klay Thompson to only nine. Surely, with James, Love, and Irving combining to score 66 points, one would have thought the result would be a Cleveland blowout. One man coming off the Golden State bench had different ideas, however.

If he were playing behind Curry, Shaun Livingston would have been Golden State's starting point guard. Rubbing a little salt in the wound for Cleveland was the fact that they had Livingston under their own roof in 2012–13.

Livingston entered the league directly out of high school, when he was selected in the first round of the 2004 NBA draft by the Los Angeles Clippers with the fourth overall pick. Considered a five-star recruit by Rivals.com, Livingston was listed as the No. 1 point guard and the No. 2 player in the nation in 2004. He committed to play college hoops at Duke but opted instead to make the jump to the NBA straight out of high school.

His career got off to a good start, as he averaged 6.3 points playing in a total of 91 games in his first two NBA seasons. In his third season, he was averaging a career-high 9.3 points when a horrible knee injury almost ended his career.

In a game against the Charlotte Bobcats on February 26, 2007, Livingston dislocated his left kneecap after landing awkwardly following a missed layup, resulting in the left leg snapping laterally. Livingston injured almost every part of his knee, tearing the anterior cruciate ligament (ACL), the posterior cruciate ligament (PCL), and the lateral meniscus; badly spraining his medial collateral ligament (MCL); and dislocating his patella and his tibiofibular joint. Livingston was told by a medical professional at the hospital that there was a chance that his leg would have to be amputated. He required months of rehabilitation to be able to walk again, and his promising career was in serious jeopardy.

It wasn't until June 16, 2008, that doctors allowed Livingston to resume basketball activities. He eventually signed a reported two-year deal with the Miami Heat on October 3, 2008. His tenure there was brief: he only appeared in four games with the Heat, averaging 2.3 points in 10.3 minutes. It wasn't much longer until he was traded to the Memphis Grizzlies along with cash considerations for a conditional 2012 second-round pick. The Grizzlies never had any actual intent on keeping him, and he was waived later that same day.

The career of the once-promising fourth overall pick seemed all but lost when he signed with the Tulsa 66ers of the NBA D-League, owned by the Oklahoma City Thunder of the NBA. After three weeks with the 66ers, Livingston signed a multi-year deal with the Thunder on March 31, 2009. It appeared this may be the chance he needed to get back in the league, but on December 22, 2009, Livingston was waived by the Thunder.

From there, he became an NBA nomad. On February 26, 2010, he signed the first of two 10-day contracts with the Washington Wizards. He was then signed by the Wizards for the remainder of the season. Following the season, Livingston signed a two-year contract worth $7 million with the Charlotte Bobcats. That stay was also short-lived: he was traded to the Milwaukee Bucks as part of a three-way deal that included the Sacramento Kings and Charlotte Bobcats on June 23, 2011. The nonstop traveling continued on June 26, 2012, when Livingston was traded to the Houston Rockets along with Jon Leuer and Jon Brockman. After being waived shortly before the season started, Livingston signed with the Washington Wizards on November 15. He was waived by the Wizards a month later. That is when Cleveland took a stab at him, claiming Livingston off waivers after releasing Donald

Sloan. He would leave there in the offseason and spend two seasons with the Brooklyn Nets.

Just when it seemed like his career might be over, the Warriors took one more chance on Livingston when they signed him to a reported three-year, $16 million contract in August of 2014. Golden State had faith in Livingston despite his being ruled out for six to eight weeks after having arthroscopic surgery on the big toe of his right foot.

Livingston finally fulfilled his potential with Golden State and managed to stay healthy, playing in 78 games in both of his seasons in Oakland. He was an excellent spark off the bench and allowed Kerr to rest Stephen Curry when needed. Livingston had stepped in and played well when Curry missed stretches of time during each of the first two rounds of the playoffs with a sore knee and ankle. In Game One of the finals, Kerr knew just when to bring him in.

With Curry and Thompson having off nights, Golden State needed someone to pick up the slack, and Livingston delivered. He scored 20 points on 8 of 10 shooting, to go along with four rebounds and three assists. He was unstoppable, and after the Cavaliers came back from 14 down in the second half to take a one-point lead, Livingston took matters into his own hands and helped the Warriors build a 17-point lead in the fourth quarter. Cleveland would not be able to recover, dropping Game One on the road, 104–89. It was a crushing blow for the Cavaliers, considering how well they defended the shooting of the Golden State starters.

Sadly for Cleveland, Game Two wouldn't be much different: the Warriors' fast-paced offense once again proved to be too much: the Cavaliers lost, 110-77, falling behind in the series, 2–0, and headed back to Cleveland for Game Three in desperation mode.

The Cavaliers actually led, 21–19, after the first quarter before the wheels came off. Love had to leave with a possible concussion after a brutal elbow from Harrison Barnes, and the Warriors rolled from there. Golden State outscored Cleveland by 10 in the second quarter and by 12 in the third before putting them away for good in the fourth, outscoring them, 28–15, in the final frame. The 33-point loss was depressing as it gets. It looked as though all hope was lost, and so were the chances of bringing an NBA championship to Cleveland. Something had to change.

That something may have been forced on coach Lue when Kevin Love was not cleared to play in Game Three back in Cleveland, remaining in concussion protocol. Lue would have to adjust his starting lineup and replace Love with veteran Richard Jefferson. Jefferson was no stranger to big moments, playing in the NBA Finals twice with the New Jersey Nets and many big games after that. He was ready, and the moment was not too big for him.

The insertion of Jefferson into the lineup was big, but the Cavaliers still needed big plays from Kyrie Irving, Tristan Thompson, and J. R. Smith, who had all been silent in the first two games, both blowout losses. Perhaps it was the home court, perhaps it was the desperation of being down two games, but regardless of what it was, the Cavaliers came out in the first quarter with all guns blazing and ran all over the Warriors. They led by as many as 22 points in the first quarter, and the roof was about to blow off the Quicken Loans Arena.

Irving finally stepped up and erupted, scoring 16 of his team's 33 first-quarter points. It was the spark they needed, and it instantly inspired the rest of the team to play better, as well. He would go on to finish with 30 points and eight assists.

Thompson also stepped it up, playing like a max-salary player for the first time all postseason. He finished with 14 big points along with 13 rebounds and clogged the middle all night long. Thompson needed this big night, because it was his playoff performance last year against Golden State that led to his max contract salary this year, and he needed to start earning it when it counted.

Perhaps the biggest disappointment for Cleveland through the first two games was Smith. For the second straight Finals, the flashy shooter had disappeared at the worst time. With Love out, they would need his scoring touch now more than ever. Smith broke out in Game Three with 20 points, connecting on five three-pointers and finally looking like the man they were counting on to help win it all.

The fourth starter to score in double digits was James, who finished with 32 points, 11 rebounds, and six assists. He had his typically stellar night, including a highlight-reel alley-oop dunk in the third quarter to put the game out of reach, as the Cavaliers rolled to a 120–90 victory. The 30-point win was exactly what they needed to get back in the series and reclaim much-needed confidence and momentum.

Perhaps even more impressive than the scoring were the hustle and defense that they showed for the first time in the series. Stephen Curry was held to just two points in the first quarter, and just 19 for the game. They also held his Splash Brother Klay Thompson to only 10 points. Draymond Green was limited to six points after scoring a game-high 28 in Game Two. If the Cavaliers could continue playing this type of defense, they could just possibly come back and win the series.

The big question on coach Lue's plate heading into Game Four at home would be who would he start at power forward? If Kevin Love passed concussion protocol, how could he possibly not start one of their three best players? On the other hand, they just won by 30 with Love on the bench all night and Jefferson starting. After being cleared to play, Love went to Lue and told him he was fine with either starting or coming off the bench, so the coach decided to stick with Jefferson.

His decision to go with Jefferson paid off: as the Cavaliers once again got off to a hot start fueled in part by the raucous crowd screaming with excitement after every play. Irving was unstoppable, as he was able to drive to the basket with ease and also play tough defense on the other end. Behind his strong play, the Cavaliers led at halftime, 55–50, and looked to have things in hand.

Everything would fall apart in the second half. Lue left Love on the bench too long, and the game would eventually get out of hand, as the Warriors built a nine-point lead early in the fourth quarter. Irving (34 points) simply couldn't do it by himself. LeBron had 25 points but turned the ball over seven times. Meanwhile, Stephen Curry finally started to heat up with 38 points. He caught fire and never let up, shooting 7 of 13 from behind the three-point arc. Curry was having a calm series until that point, but one asinine Cleveland fan thought it would be smart to tweet nasty things about the Golden State star's sister and young daughter, which was enough to catch national attention and piss off Curry to the point that he had all the motivation he needed to end his shooting slump. Mix in some hard feelings about the widely ridiculed debut of his new shoe, and Curry had all the ammunition he needed for a big night.

Klay Thompson also shot the lights out, hitting four of nine three-point attempts and scoring 25 points overall. Perhaps the hardest pill to swallow came from former Cavalier Anderson Varejao, who only played four minutes but managed to grab three straight offensive rebounds to keep the ball away from Cleveland at a pivotal point late in the third quarter. The Cavaliers were only down, 74–73, at the time, but Andy made sure they weren't getting the ball back, despite three straight Golden State misses. Final score: Golden State 108, Cleveland 97. The Cavaliers' hopes for a championship were now on life support.

Maybe only thing giving them hope as they headed back to Oracle Arena for Game Five was that Warriors star power forward Draymond Green would be suspended for that game. The ruling that came down from the NBA after some seriously dirty plays throughout the playoffs had him one strike away from a suspension, to begin with. Green took a swipe at LeBron and looked as though he hit James in the groin, or at least attempted to do so during a heated exchange late in the fourth quarter of Game Four. After reviewing the tape, the NBA felt it was enough to suspend him for the next game. So if the Warriors wanted to put away the Cavaliers in five games, they would need to do so without their resident bad boy.

In Game Three of the Western finals, Green kicked Thunder center Steven Adams in the groin. The foul was later upgraded from a Flagrant Foul 1 to a Flagrant 2, and he was fined $25,000. That put the NBA front office on high alert, and they began to watch his every move the rest of the postseason. His tangle with James late in Game Four with the outcome no longer in doubt—in which Green swung his arm and appeared to make contact with James's groin—was the last straw. Green was assessed a Flagrant 1 for contact that was ruled unnecessary and retaliatory, and James was given a technical foul for taunting. Having accumulated his fourth flagrant foul point in the playoffs, Green was suspended for Game Five. The Cavaliers would have their glimmer of hope.

On neosportsinsiders.com, I had compared this Golden State Warriors team to the Detroit Pistons of 1988 to 1990. Known as the "Bad Boys," Isiah Thomas led them to back-to-back NBA championships. Part of my comparison was based on the similarities between Stephen Curry and Isiah Thomas. They were each the best shooter in the game at the time, along with a great backcourt teammate. Curry had Klay Thompson, while Thomas had the legendary Joe Dumars. The Pistons were eventually unseated by the Chicago Bulls, and the rest is history.

One big comparison that stood out the most was between power forwards Draymond Green and Dennis Rodman. Both were volatile players who could outrebound anyone and often found themselves in the midst of chaos and controversy. They were hated by opposing fans and players, and loved by their own.

Draymond Green grew up in Saginaw, Michigan, where he became a fan of the game. He played basketball in high school at Saginaw and performed extremely well, leading them to state championships in his junior and senior seasons.

Green played his college ball at Michigan State, where he finished as the school's all-time leading rebounder. He was named the Big Ten Player of the Year as a senior and became one of three players in Michigan State history with over 1,000 points and 1,000 rebounds. It was a great four-year stint at Michigan State, capped off by two Final Four appearances and a Big Ten Tournament Championship in 2012. Golden State noticed what kind of game changer Green was and drafted him 35th overall in the 2012 NBA draft.

His heart and hustle led him to become one of the toughest and best players in the NBA as he helped lead the Warriors to the NBA title in 2014–15, his third season in the league. He was voted runner-up in both the Defensive Player of the Year Award and the Most Improved Player Award categories. It was also during Game Six of the NBA Finals against Cleveland that he showed his versatility and hustle when he started at center in place of Andrew Bogut. The moved paid off: he became just the sixth player in NBA history to record a triple-double in an NBA Finals-clinching game with 16 points, 11 rebounds, and 10 assists.

In appreciation of Green's contributions to the championship season, the Warriors didn't hesitate to reward their newest superstar. On July 9, 2015, Green signed a new five-year, $82 million contract. He rewarded their faith in him with a great regular season, including an All-Star Game appearance. He became the first player in NBA history to record 1,000 points, 500 rebounds, 500 assists, 100 steals, and 100 blocks in a season. Green was selected to the All-NBA Second Team. He again finished runner-up for the Defensive Player of the Year award and was named to the All-Defensive Team with the second-most votes.

His absence for Game Five gave the Cavaliers hope they could pull off a giant upset and send the series back to Cleveland.

Not that it would need it in any way, but Game Five got an added bit of drama the day before the game when Klay Thompson and LeBron James took subtle digs at each other at a press conference. This was not the first time Thompson had something to say during the series: he had blamed his poor play in a Game Three loss on what he claimed was a dirty foul by Timofey Mozgov.

"Guys talk trash in this league all the time. I'm just kind of shocked some guys take it so personal," Thompson said. "I don't know how [James] feels. But obviously people have feelings, and people's feelings get hurt even if they're called a bad word. I guess his feelings just got hurt. I mean, we've all been called plenty of bad words on the basketball court before. Some guys just react to it differently."

James was almost amused when he replied, "My goodness. I'm not going to comment on what Klay said, because I know where it can go from this sit-in. It's so hard to take the high road. I've been doing it for thirteen years. It's so hard to continue to do it, and I'm going to do it again."

All drama aside, the loss of Green for Game Five was a big deal, since the Warriors had only played without him three times in the regular season, losing all three times. That alone was big considering they only lost nine games all season. The Warriors would have to work past it, or they would be traveling across the country back to Cleveland for a Game Six.

An instant classic would develop, as Klay Thompson and LeBron James would take their verbal sparring to the court for a first-half shootout. Defense was out the window; both men went off, scoring almost every time they touched the ball. At the end of the first half, it was 61–61. LeBron was the James of old—his jump shot was working, and he didn't hesitate to drive the lane at will. He finished the first half with 25 points and kept the Cavaliers in it every time the Warriors and Thompson, who had 26 first-half points of his own, looked to be pulling away.

The crowd at Oracle Arena was hostile and would boo James loudly every time he touched the ball, but that just fueled him more, and he continued to light it up in the second half, eventually finishing with 41 points, 16 rebounds, seven assists, three steals, and three blocks while helping the Cavaliers stave off elimination with a stunning 112–97 win. It was a performance that had fans and media alike harkening back to some of his greatest games ever, such as his overtime classic against the Detroit Pistons in Game Five of the 2007 Eastern Conference Finals on the road, and his Game Six of the 2012 Eastern Conference Finals with the Miami Heat in Boston to avoid elimination. His performance in the latter game is credited with finally getting him over the championship hump. Perhaps this was the game James needed to have to get Cleveland over the championship hump.

As greatly as James played, he wasn't even the best player on the court that night, because Kyrie Irving had what was easily the greatest game of his professional career. Irving also finished with 41 points but scored his in a way that drove a stake through the heart of the Warriors. Every time it looked as though Golden State was on the verge of coming back, or taking over, Irving would hit a big shot and give the momentum right back to Cleveland. He would not allow the Cavaliers to die, as he and James willed them to victory.

The Warriors' dynamic duo of Klay Thompson (37 points) and Stephen Curry (25) also had great games, but it simply wasn't enough. The loss of Green was readily apparent, because they lacked the same defensive intensity they had in the first four games and couldn't stop James from driving the lane.

Everywhere the Cavaliers and their fans turned, all they heard was that no team had ever come back from a 3–1 deficit in the NBA Finals. They refused to listen to the odds and never lost hope that it could happen. It might have helped matters that some said the curse was broken the prior weekend when the Lake Erie Monsters won the AHL's Calder Cup in dramatic fashion over the Hershey Bears, 1–0, on a goal with 1.2 seconds left in overtime. Perhaps that was the mojo the Cavaliers needed to get over the hump and buck history.

In a season that seemed to have a dark spot to go with every bright spot, Game Five would be no different. Cleveland would have a cross-country trip and two off days to figure out what to do with the struggling Kevin Love, who had just two points and three rebounds in a game in which he should have been able to exploit a mismatch.

The issues with Love aside, there was no mistaking the Cavaliers had stolen back the momentum and were ready to shock the world by forcing a Game Seven. The crowd would start filling into Quicken Loans Arena hours before the game at a rapid pace, and as Cavaliers fans dreamed of an epic comeback and were ready to cheer and stand all game, Stephen Curry's wife was having a quite different pregame experience.

Ayesha Curry had been shown in the crowd along with Stephen's parents after almost every single big shot her husband made over the last two seasons. She was a media darling, as was her daughter Riley, whom Stephen brought up on stage with him at press conferences. That would change when Ayesha Curry made some ill-advised tweets on a night that she won't soon forget.

She started tweeting about ten minutes before the tip-off for Game Six, and they weren't positive signs of how the night would go for her and her husband. Her first tweet claimed that the bus that takes family and friends over to the arena was held up outside of the gate and they weren't allowed in. She went on to claim that her own father was stopped by police and not allowed in, claiming he was being racially profiled. It should be pointed out that the game took place only days after the deadly shootings in an Orlando night club that caused forty-nine innocent people to lose their lives, so security was going to be extra tight anywhere a large crowd was gathering. She also complained in a later tweet that her cousin wasn't let into a casino because he was wearing Warriors gear. She kept at it a few minutes after that by tweeting a picture of the bus sitting outside of Progressive Field still waiting to get into Quicken Loans Arena.

While things weren't going well for Ayesha before the game, things would be even worse for her husband once the game got underway. He picked up two quick fouls in the first quarter as the Cavaliers ran out to an 11–0 lead and looked to have their foot on the gas pedal. Everything was going right for the Cavs: Tristan Thompson seemed to rip down every single rebound, and James, Irving, and Smith didn't seem to miss a shot. Kevin Love was hampered by two quick fouls himself in under two minutes and had to sit on the bench for the rest of the quarter.

It was a dominant quarter for the Cavaliers, as they forced turnovers, hit every big shot, and attacked the boards. It was clear the intensity level was off the charts, since LeBron had told the team before the game that they just needed to trust and follow him and he would get them to Game Seven. They believed in him and it showed, as they crushed the Warriors' spirit in the first quarter and led by as many as 22 at one point. Cleveland closed out the quarter with a 31–11 lead and seemed to be destined for the Game Seven showdown.

Curry would re-enter the in the second quarter, as would Love. Golden State would climb back into the game when both Curry and Klay Thompson started hitting three-pointers. It didn't help matters when Love picked up his third foul and had to go right back to the bench less than two minutes into the quarter. The Warriors cut the lead to 11 before the Cavaliers went on a run to take a 59–43 halftime lead. They were just 24 minutes away from forcing a Game Seven back in Oakland.

Cleveland appeared to put the game away when they went up by 24 points, 70–46, their largest lead of the game, halfway through the third quarter. The Warriors then made one last push and started to hit three-pointers from everywhere on the court, going on a 25–10 run. Klay Thompson hit three consecutive three-pointers in the last 90 seconds of the third quarter, cutting the lead down to 80–71 heading into the final frame.

The Cavaliers had been up by 20 only minutes earlier, and the panic may have been setting in when LeBron James took matters into his own hands. During the timeout between quarters, the nerves were obvious, because a once-massive lead was cut down to single digits. Mix in the fact that it was a year to the day that the Cavaliers had lost the 2015 finals to Golden State, and it was easy to see why everyone started to get nervous. LeBron again reminded his team to trust and follow him and he would get them to Game Seven.

James did just that, flashing back to his epic performance against Detroit in Game Five of the 2007 Eastern Conference

Finals, when he took over the game by scoring 29 of his team's last 30 points, including the final 25. Against Golden State in Game Six, James would do it again, scoring or assisting on 27 consecutive points and 35 of 36 during a stretch spanning the third and fourth quarters. It was an incredible effort that allowed the Cavaliers to put the Warriors away for good and walk away with a 115–101 victory. James scored 17 in the fourth and 41 for the game along with 11 assists and eight rebounds. His second consecutive 41-point outing helped improve his record in elimination games to 9–8.

Cleveland's pressure defense and intensified effort seemed to be getting to the Warriors once-high-octane, shoot-the-lights-out offense. While Stephen Curry (30 points) and Klay Thompson (25) remained hot in Game Six, they received little support. Andre Iguodala suffered back spasms and became a nonfactor, scoring only five points. Harrison Barnes's shooting slump continued, as he missed all eight of his field-goal attempts. Draymond Green did help, scoring eight points and pulling down 10 rebounds, but it wasn't enough to make the difference he promised to make. Green had stated earlier that if he had played in Game Five, the Warriors would have put it away at home.

Shaun Livingston, who had a coming-out party in Game One, had now been shut down, as coach Lue and the Cleveland defense had made the needed adjustments. They held Livingston to only three points on 1 of 6 shooting in 21-plus minutes. The Warriors were nervous and having to scramble for answers as the deeper bench of the Cavaliers was peaking at the right time.

The game did not end without the requisite drama, as Stephen Curry had his own meltdown of epic proportions. He fouled out of the game with 4:22 left and then lost his mind, cursing at the officials, followed by taking his famed mouthpiece out and throwing it at a fan sitting courtside. Suddenly, the NBA's sweetheart and face of the league had become a villain. He stormed off the court, swearing at everyone and continuing to make a scene as he headed back to the locker room. After the game, he gave this explanation for his behavior: "I don't think I fouled either Kyrie or LeBron on the last two fouls called on me. It was obviously frustrating fouling out in the fourth quarter of a clinching game and not being out there with my teammates. It got the best of me, but I'll be all right for Game Seven."

Steve Kerr, a coach known for usually taking the high road, showed his frustration at the postgame press conference: "As the MVP of the league, we're talking about these touch fouls in the NBA Finals. I'm happy he threw his mouthpiece."

As the final seconds ticked off the clock, the crowd at Quicken Loans Arena, along with the thousands of fans packed outside of it partying at Gate Way Plaza, went nuts with excitement. The once-impossible dream of ending a fifty-two-year championship drought while coming back from a 3–1 deficit suddenly seemed very much in reach. It was the biggest win in franchise history and one that not many in the national media saw coming. Michelle Beadle, the co-host of ESPN's *SportsNation* show, had actually claimed that she was so confident the Cavaliers had no chance to come back down 3–1, she would eat a book if they did. (Logically enough, the book she chose to eat was *The Cleveland Cavaliers: A History of the Wine & Gold* by yours truly. She was suddenly staring at a tough meal to digest.)

Cleveland had fought back against all odds from the edge of elimination to reach the brink of history. In the end, James's 41 points were a symphony, a ballet that could only be performed by a champion, while his running mate, Kyrie Irving, continued to ascend as he put in 23 points. These two former top overall picks now had the Cavaliers on the brink of doing what no other team had ever done in the history of the NBA with absolutely no margin for error. The lights were on bright, and the stars were shining. Irving and James had the most to do with the epic comeback, but they weren't doing it completely alone. Tristan Thompson scored 15 points, yanked down 16 rebounds, and was a dominating presence in the paint in Game Six. When Thompson was on, the Cavaliers won, a formula that had been proven to be successful dating back to the 2015 NBA Finals. J. R. Smith also helped the cause with 14 points. Cleveland had saved its season for the second time in three days and now headed back to Oracle Arena in Oakland to complete the miracle.

While Cleveland fans were celebrating in the streets of Cleveland, Ayesha Curry was tweeting away. She went on a tirade before wisely deleting it all. One of the tweets detailed how the NBA is fixed. A league that had made her and her husband millionaires, a league that had named her husband NBA MVP two seasons in a row and that had sent him to back-to-back NBA Finals, was suddenly fixed? She would later try and take back the tweet by saying that the she shouldn't have tweeted in the heat of the moment, and that she was only upset because police at Quicken Loans Arena had racially profiled her father. She went on to claim the police had made him remove his credentials and tried to arrest him. She wasn't done yet, explaining how she was okay with the Warriors losing the game but was upset by people coming at her family for no reason. It was something she didn't stand for. So apparently she enjoyed the fame and money the NBA and its fans had brought to her family, but not the criticism that sometimes came with it.

All the drama and tweeting aside, the comeback was one win away from being complete, and despite the fact that the game would be in Oakland, the city of Cleveland would not miss out on the action. Team owner Dan Gilbert opened up Quicken Loans Arena once again for an official Cavaliers watch party. The tickets went on sale the morning after the Game Six win and sold out in less than ten minutes. With the excitement Cleveland fans had for this big game, they could have opened up both Progressive Field and First Energy Stadium for watch parties and filled them up. The euphoria was at an all-time high, and for good reason.

CHAPTER 10

Game Seven

THERE ARE NO TWO BIGGER words in all of sports than *Game Seven*, and the Golden State Warriors and Cleveland Cavaliers were set to do battle in one on June 19, 2016, at Oracle Arena in Oakland, California. What once seemed like a pipe dream was now reality for the Cavaliers, as they attempted to end the misery of every Cleveland sports fan. The moment was now, and the chance of a lifetime had arrived for the fifteen men in uniform, and the several coaches under the Cleveland Cavaliers banner, to go down as immortals in Cleveland sports lore. For LeBron James, this was the reason he came back; and all the aggravation, drama, and doubts would finally go away and all would be forgiven with just one more win. It may have been Klay Thompson's insults that finally put him over the edge, but whatever it was, he was playing the best basketball of his life over the previous two games and just needed one more Herculean effort to end the curse and achieve redemption.

The team had taken things one game at a time throughout the playoffs. They had a life-size puzzle built of the Larry O'Brien Trophy with sixteen different pieces to rip off. It was much like the one seen in the movie *Major League*, also about a Cleveland team overcoming a curse. Each time they won a game, they would remove a section of the puzzle. The last four pieces were reserved for Kevin Love, LeBron James, Kyrie Irving, and Tyronn Lue. In symbolic fashion, Love removed piece number 13, which came after the Game Three victory, a game he didn't even play in, but they wanted to keep his confidence up. They wanted him to always feel like a member of the team even when outside forces, in the media and in bad luck, seemed to keep him down. They knew he would get his moment soon enough, and Game Seven was about to provide just that.

In a small bit of irony, it was on Father's Day in 2014 that James played his last game with the Miami Heat, when the San Antonio Spurs bounced them from the NBA Finals in just five games. Here it was, two years later, once again Father's Day, and he was on the cusp of history. It was a Hollywood script that just needed an epic ending. The hometown boy, who tried to save a city and bring it its long-awaited championship, leaves and wins it elsewhere, and then comes back to try to win it again and keep his original promise. It was a story written by the sports gods!

Going into the final game, there had been eighteen Game Sevens played in NBA Finals history, with the road team going a paltry 3–15. The last home team to lose an NBA Finals Game Seven was the Seattle SuperSonics in 1978. The Washington Bullets was the team to knock off the Lenny Wilkens-led Sonics. Ironically, neither team currently existed under those names, as the SuperSonics left Seattle and became the Oklahoma City Thunder, while the Washington Bullets became the Washington

Wizards. However you sliced it or by whatever name you wanted to call it, Game Seven did not look good for the away team.

The last time a Cleveland sports team played in a Game Seven for a chance at a championship was in 1997, when the Indians faced the Florida Marlins. That year was an impossible dream, because the Indians had won just 86 games before heating up in the playoffs and riding rookie pitcher Jaret Wright's arm to the brink of World Series glory. The Indians came within two outs of winning the title in the bottom of the ninth, before Jose Mesa blew the save and a furious Marlins rally would eventually win the game and give Cleveland even more heartbreak.

That night in Florida would live in infamy as one of the hardest nights in Cleveland sports history. The town had suffered so much, their Browns losing three AFC title games between 1986 and 1989. Once they lost because of an improbable last-second, 98-yard drive by John Elway to tie the game, then a field goal by Rich Karlis in overtime that many to this day said was no good. Their heartache would only compound itself the next year, as once again they lost to Denver after a last-second fumble by Earnest Byner on the goal line kept them from tying the game. The worst pain for Browns fans would be in 1995, when Art Modell moved the team to Baltimore in perhaps one of the most shocking incidents in sports history.

The Cavaliers were no stranger to heartache themselves. In 1989, Michael Jordan hit a last-second shot over Craig Ehlo to knock them out of the playoffs. That play was immortalized by a Gatorade commercial. The city didn't want to be like Mike, they didn't want to cheer John Elway, and they wanted to burn Art Modell and Jose Mesa. They had been through, and seen, enough. There was no need for films, commercials, or television shows to remind them of their misery: they lived with it every day and were ready to turn it all around.

As the ball tipped off in Oracle Arena that fateful Father's Day evening, the drama in Oakland was palpable. It was easy to tell both teams were tense, as shots were being forced and turnovers were occurring at a rapid pace. LeBron James, who was coming off two amazing efforts, looked tense and committed three early turnovers. He would eventually shake the nerves and become the game's most dominant player of the night. Nerves also got the best of regular-season MVP Stephen Curry, as well, as he picked up two fouls in the early going. The first quarter would remain tight and end with Cleveland up, 23–22.

The second quarter would be a different story, as Golden State became hot from beyond the three-point arc to take a 49–42 halftime lead. The Warriors hit many open looks and drained 10 of 21 three-point attempts in the first half. Draymond Green went 5-for-5 during that stretch. On the other hand, the Cavaliers struggled from downtown, hitting only 1 of 14 attempts. It looked like the gas tank might finally be empty and the miracle comeback might come up just short.

Cleveland came out like a team on a mission in the second half, as J. R. Smith hit his first three shots, including two three-pointers to get them back in the game. The Cavaliers would continue to push and in a huge turnaround took a 70-63 lead, silencing the Golden State crowd. The momentum shift was clear, and Cleveland looked to be putting away the Warriors with one of the patented second-half runs that they had been using all postseason.

Golden State responded with a run of their own, complete with a terrible foul call on LeBron James that gave Draymond Green three foul shots. Not only didn't James foul him, it shouldn't have been called a shooting foul. However, the men with the whistles saw it differently and awarded Green the three shots, and he promptly sank all three. That call turned the game back in the

Warriors' favor, and they would come back to lead by one point, 76–75, heading into the fourth quarter.

It was only appropriate that a Game Seven played between the league's two best teams would come down to a final quarter with only a point separating them. It would stay tight into the final two minutes. Suffocating defense by Cleveland kept the Warriors scoreless for the last four-and-a-half minutes of the game and kept Cleveland fans glued to their TV screens with their stomach in knots and a flicker of hope remaining.

With the game tied at 89 and just under two minutes left, Andre Iguodala had the chance to erase what had been a terrible shooting game for him. He broke away on a fast break and looked to have a wide-open layup to give the Warriors the lead until "Flight 23" LeBron James came out of nowhere to block his shot from behind and get the ball back for the Cavaliers. LeBron had done it again, coming through with a crucial block to turn the momentum, giving the entire city of Cleveland a reason to believe.

On the other side of the court, Kyrie Irving pounded the ball outside of the three-point arc waiting for a shot to open up, and when it didn't, he created his own. With the hopes of Cleveland raising his feet and the belief in better days straightening his arms and elbows, Irving spotted up and sank one from deep. His cold-blooded 25-footer with 53 seconds remaining gave the Cavaliers a 92–89 lead. In a moment that seemed to stand still in time, the fifth-year player from Duke who was chosen in 2011 to turn around a burned franchise came through at the most important time.

Kevin Love, Irving's Big Three teammate, then stepped up when Stephen Curry tried desperately to get open for a game-tying three. Love, who was playing an excellent defensive game, wouldn't allow Curry an inch to breathe. With Love right in his face, Curry chucked up a desperate three with 31 seconds left that was never close. For Curry, it was the final blow in a dreadful Game Seven that saw him score just 17 points, going a pitiful 4 of 14 from beyond the arc. Love had done his job, and after two seasons of people doubting him, he came through when he absolutely had to. Love and Irving both got their chance to shine in the biggest moments, and they performed brilliantly.

In what was almost poetic justice, the final shot, the final blow and the touch on the long-awaited championship, came from the hometown boy, with LeBron James splitting a pair of free throws in the final seconds to give the Cavaliers a four-point lead and put the game away, along with the curse!

Like a desert's craving for water, LeBron James and the 2016 Cleveland Cavaliers quenched Cleveland's thirst for a world championship. James would finish with 27 points, 11 rebounds, 11 assists, three blocks, and two steals. It was a triple-double for the King, but his biggest play was the blocked shot of Iguodala that saved a championship, a season, and an entire city. The weight had finally been lifted from his shoulders. Redemption was his, and the NBA writers would recognize that by naming him series MVP.

Klay Thompson, whose mocking of LeBron after the Warriors were up 3–1 may have turned the entire series around and woken up the beast, went out with a whimper as he finished with 14 points, including just 2 of 10 from long range. Draymond Green did his best, scoring an impressive 32 points with 15 rebounds, but it simply wasn't enough.

You couldn't help but become emotional watching as the season of dreams had truly become a reality. Richard Jefferson, the cagey veteran who provided so much inspiration for his teammates down the stretch, once again played a key role by grabbing nine big rebounds off the bench in 25 minutes. J. R. Smith finished with only 12 points, but they were all huge. Kevin Love had been embattled all year, but his presence was felt in Game Seven, as he yanked down 14 rebounds and the Cavaliers were plus-19 when he was on the court.

The biggest shot of the game was made by Kyrie Irving, and it was just one of many big shots he sank all night long. Irving would finish with 26 points, providing LeBron James with that number two scoring punch he craved. James had it in Miami with Dwyane Wade as he won two titles, and he now had it with Irving; and because of it, Cleveland had become "Believeland" after all. Carl Jung once said, "I am not what has happened to me, I am what I choose to become." For Cleveland, they chose to become CHAMPIONS!

About the Author

VINCE MCKEE IS ONE OF the top sportswriters in Northeast Ohio. He is the author of eight books on Cleveland sports, along with his duties as Senior VP of Sponsorship with neosportsinsiders.com. His work has been featured on ESPN television and in *SLAM* Magazine, along with *Drennan Live* and the *Cleveland Plain Dealer* and many other media outlets. Vince speaks about his journey at churches, schools, and libraries statewide to spread the message of believing in yourself. For bookings and feedback, he can be reached at coachvin14@yahoo.com. You can follow him on Twitter at Vince The Author. Vince currently lives in North Olmsted, Ohio, with his wife, Emily, and daughter, Maggie. Baby number two is on the way in September 2016.